WORDSWORTH
AND
COLERIDGE

LYRICAL BALLADS

1798

EDITED BY

W. J. B. OWEN

Professor of English
McMaster University

SECOND EDITION

OXFORD UNIVERSITY PRESS
1969

Oxford University Press, Ely House, London W. 1

GLASGOW NEW YORK TORONTO MELBOURNE WELLINGTON
CAPE TOWN SALISBURY IBADAN NAIROBI LUSAKA ADDIS ABABA
BOMBAY CALCUTTA MADRAS KARACHI LAHORE DACCA
KUALA LUMPUR SINGAPORE HONG KONG TOKYO

© *Oxford University Press 1969*

First edition 1967
Second edition 1969

Printed in Great Britain by
The Camelot Press Ltd., London and Southampton

NOTE ON THE SECOND EDITION

In this edition I have corrected a few misprints; added some bibliographical references and explanatory material; and revised references to Wordsworth's published correspondence so as to take account of the new Oxford edition currently in progress.

W. J. B. OWEN

PREFACE

THIS edition of *Lyrical Ballads*, 1798, replaces that by Harold Littledale, first published in 1911 and now out of print. It attempts to put before the reader a reliable text and to make use of some of the more important scholarly discoveries and emphases of recent years.

My Introduction deals as briefly as possible with what is known and surmised about the motives for and the processes of publishing the book in 1798, and discusses more fully the poetry in its relation to the traditions from which it sprang. I have indulged in a certain amount of biographical inference in the matter of Wordsworth's motives for writing the experimental poems of 1798, and I have deliberately avoided the vexed and possibly not very meaningful question of personal symbolism in *The Ancient Mariner*. The difficult problems of aesthetics raised by Wordsworth's Advertisement of 1798 and Prefaces of 1800 and 1802 have been discussed elsewhere, at a length inappropriate to an edition of this kind.[1]

The Commentary draws frequently upon remarks on their work made by the authors themselves, and in particular it reprints, almost always in full, the notes to Wordsworth's poems commonly called the Fenwick notes since they were

---

[1] W. J. B. Owen, *Wordsworth's Preface to* Lyrical Ballads (Copenhagen, 1957); and *Wordsworth as Critic* (Toronto, 1969).

dictated by the poet in 1843 to Isabella Fenwick. They are often garrulous and sometimes inaccurate, but they are the best single body of commentary on the poems that I know. My text of these notes is from the transcript by Edward Quillinan and Dora Quillinan (*née* Wordsworth) in the Wordsworth Library, Grasmere, and therefore differs occasionally from other reprints. I have added punctuation where it seemed absolutely necessary, expanded the ampersand to 'and', and introduced one emendation (in the note to *We are Seven*). I have also included references to the classification of Wordsworth's poems which he introduced in the collected edition of 1815 and defended in the Preface to that edition. In some cases the references are merely formal, but in others (see, for instance, the notes to *Goody Blake* and *The Thorn*) they throw light on Wordsworth's intentions.

I have followed the example of Littledale by printing in an Appendix the Preface to *Lyrical Ballads*, 1800, and adding as footnotes the variant readings of the Preface of 1802. The texts have been newly collated with, I believe, some gain in accuracy.

I am indebted to the Trustees of the Wordsworth Library, Grasmere, for permission to use the manuscript text of the Fenwick notes and to quote a few sentences from an unpublished manuscript; to Cornell University Library; and to McMaster University for research grants.

W. J. B. OWEN

CONTENTS

Introduction	vii
Select Bibliography and List of Abbreviations	xxxvii
Lyrical Ballads	1
Advertisement	3
Contents	5
Text	7
Errata	117
Commentary	118
Appendix	153

INTRODUCTION

I

THE prime cause of the appearance of *Lyrical Ballads* in 1798 seems to have been the chronic poverty of its authors.[1] 'In the Spring of the year 1798', Wordsworth said in 1843, '[Coleridge], my Sister, and myself started from Alfoxden, pretty late in the afternoon, with a view to visit Linton and the Valley of Stones near it, and as our united funds were very small, we agreed to defray the expense of the tour by writing a Poem to be sent to the New Monthly Magazine. . . . Accordingly we set off . . . and in the course of this walk was planned the Poem of The Ancient Mariner' (I.F. to *We are Seven*, p. 135 below). No one, so far as I know, has ever challenged the financial motive behind the publication, and indeed Wordsworth confirmed it when he grumbled over the tone of Southey's review of the book in the *Critical Review* for October 1798;[2] but the statement of 1843 is only one of many confusing accounts of facts and of the contributory motives which went to the making of *Lyrical Ballads*. The relevant walking tour took place in November 1797, not in the spring of 1798, and several editors have printed the note accordingly.[3]

[1] The first section of this introduction is indebted in a general way to Mark L. Reed, 'Wordsworth, Coleridge, and the "Plan" of the *Lyrical Ballads*', *U.T.Q.*, xxxiv (1965), 238–53.

[2] 'Southey . . . knew that I published those poems for money and money alone. He knew that money was of importance to me. If he could not conscientiously have spoken differently of the volume, he ought to have declined the task of reviewing it' (*E.Y.*, pp. 267–8).

[3] The reading 'In the autumn of 1797' printed by, e.g. Dykes Campbell, *Poetical Works of . . . Coleridge* (London, 1893, &c.), p. 594, and Lowes, p. 222, seems to derive from a sophistication by Christopher Wordsworth in his *Memoirs of William Wordsworth* (London, 1851), i. 107. Hutchinson, p. xlvii, prints 'On Nov. 13, 1797', without comment.

That *The Ancient Mariner* was planned during a walking tour in November 1797 is confirmed by a letter of Dorothy Wordsworth dated 20 November 1797: 'We have been on another tour: we set out last Monday evening [13 November] at half past four. The evening was dark and cloudy; we went eight miles, William and Coleridge employing themselves in laying the plan of a ballad, to be published with some pieces of William's' (*E.Y.*, p. 194). According to Coleridge's note of 1817 to *The Ancient Mariner*, 'this Poem was planned and in part composed' 'on a delightful walk from Nether Stowey to Dulverton' (*C.P.W.*, i. 196). In another letter, not dated more precisely than 'Nov. 1797' (*E.Y.*, Letter 76, p. 194), Dorothy describes a walk to Lynmouth and the Valley of Stones through Porlock. Whether these two fragmentary letters describe two 'tours', the one to Lynmouth (Letter 76) and back, and another, beginning 13 November (Letter 77), to Dulverton and back (Coleridge's note), which Wordsworth telescoped into one tour to Lynmouth returning via Dulverton (I.F. to *We are Seven*), or whether the fragments describe to two correspondents the one tour which Wordsworth accurately described but misdated in the I.F. note, is uncertain.[1]

Why did Wordsworth attribute the genesis of *Lyrical Ballads* to the financial needs of a tour in the spring of 1798? On 5 March 1798 Dorothy reports that the Wordsworths have to give up their tenancy of Alfoxden; 'if the poems bring in any thing considerable', they may well visit the Hutchinsons in Sockburn (*E.Y.*, p. 200). On 6 March Wordsworth repeats the news of their impending departure: 'What may be our

---

[1] Mrs. Moorman, *Early Years*, pp. 346–7, postulates two tours and Wordsworth's confusion of them. For the contrary view, see Lowes, p. 529, n. 5. Dorothy's phrase 'another tour' in Letter 77 is consistent with, but does not prove, the first opinion.

INTRODUCTION ix

destination I cannot say. If we can raise the money, we shall make a tour on foot; probably through Wales, and northwards' (*E.Y.*, p. 211). But on 11 March (*E.Y.*, p. 213) he has decided to accompany Coleridge to Germany; and, perhaps two days later, he is approaching Cottle,[1] through Coleridge, with the intention of publishing, not *Lyrical Ballads*, but *The Borderers*, *Salisbury Plain* (containing *The Female Vagrant*, and the basis of the later *Guilt and Sorrow*), his 'Tale of a Woman' (meaning, probably, *The Ruined Cottage*, the basis of *The Excursion*, Book I), and 'a few others' (*C.L.*, i. 399–400). The financial arrangements proposed are uncertain as to amount, but precise as to date, as if Wordsworth were now seeking funds to support either the visit to Germany, or his immediate needs after leaving Alfoxden, or both. March 1798, therefore, may well have been associated in Wordsworth's mind with projects for publishing which would ease his finances and assist with a tour in Britain, a visit to Germany, or both.

In late November 1797 it had been proposed to publish *The Ancient Mariner* 'with some pieces of William's'. The known or conjectured dates of most of Wordsworth's contributions to *Lyrical Ballads* do not suggest that these 'pieces' were those later published in the book: most of the *Lyrical Ballads* were written in and after early March 1798. The 'pieces' may therefore well be those on behalf of which Coleridge enquired of Cottle on 13 March 1798. Indeed, the only contributions to *Lyrical Ballads* by Wordsworth which are known certainly to have been in existence at the very

[1] Joseph Cottle (1770–1853), Bristol printer, publisher, would-be poet, friend of Wordsworth and Coleridge, and author of the unreliable *Early Recollections, chiefly relating to Samuel Taylor Coleridge* (London, 1837; a later version, *Reminiscences of... Coleridge and... Southey*, 1847), which gives a general and obscure picture of the negotiations dealt with here.

beginning of March 1798 are: *Lines left upon a Seat* . . ., *The Female Vagrant, Lines written near Richmond, Old Man Travelling*, and *The Convict*. Wordsworth had not been idle in the period November 1797–March 1798, but he had been concerned with the revision of his tragedy *The Borderers* and with attempts to have it performed in London (*E.Y.*, pp. 194–7), with the expansion of *The Ruined Cottage* (*E.Y.*, p. 199), and with 1,300 lines of *The Recluse* (or *The Prelude*) (*E.Y.*, pp. 212, 214), not with *Lyrical Ballads*. Moreover, in the middle of the same period, Coleridge proposed to sell *The Ancient Mariner* to *The Monthly Magazine* (*C.L.*, i. 368; 6 January 1798), as if the notion of joint publication had by that date been abandoned, until it reappears in mid-March with the proposal to print 'Our two Tragedies' (*Osorio* and *The Borderers*) together (*C.L.*, i. 400); Cottle (*Reminiscences*, p. 126) says that he offered the poets 'thirty guineas each . . . for their two tragedies'.

Fairly early in March, however, Wordsworth began a considerable output of verse which was to end only with *Tintern Abbey* (July 1798) and which would comprise the bulk of the new material in *Lyrical Ballads* as well as the similarly conceived *Peter Bell*; it perhaps includes the 'few other' poems he had offered Cottle in mid-March (*C.L.*, i. 400). Of these new poems, *Lines written in early Spring* presumably dates from March or April; *Lines written at a small Distance* . . . from early March (perhaps 6, 8, or 9 March; see the note to the poem); *Simon Lee* perhaps from March;[1] *The Thorn* from March (*Journals*, i. 13; 19 March 1798); *Expostulation and Reply* and *The Tables Turned*, if they were suggested by Hazlitt's visit to Coleridge, must

---

[1] So Hutchinson, on the basis of *Journals*, i. 12 (10 March 1798): 'the old man at the top of the hill gathering furze'. There seems no proof that the old man was the model for Simon Lee.

INTRODUCTION   xi

have been written during or after the period late May–early June. Other poems are not dated more precisely than that they were written at Alfoxden: *Goody Blake, Anecdote for Fathers, We are Seven, The Last of the Flock, The Mad Mother, The Idiot Boy, The Complaint of a Forsaken Indian Woman*; as there is no evidence for the existence of these before 1798, they probably belong to the first half of that year.[1] The precise dates are, indeed, not very important for our purpose; what is clear is that, as Wordsworth wrote to Cottle on 12 April, 'I have gone on very rapidly adding to my stock of poetry' (*E.Y.*, p. 215), and that, as Reed observes, the additions were largely poems written in the experimental vein which is canvassed in the Advertisement of 1798 and the Preface of 1800.[2]

By early April, the poets have abandoned the project of publishing their tragedies through Cottle; Wordsworth's

[1] Reed (p. 245) proposes to date *Goody Blake* in March, apparently because Wordsworth wished to borrow its source, Erasmus Darwin's *Zoonomia*, from Cottle in February or March, and was ready to return to Cottle books he had finished with in mid-March 1798. But we do not know that these included Darwin, which in the event was not returned until 9 May (*E.Y.*, pp. 199, 215, 218).

[2] Reed, pp. 245, 249. Cottle (*Reminiscences*, p. 132) says that he met Wordsworth on a visit to Stowey at a date which cannot be determined but which may have been in late March or early April 1798 (Moorman, *Early Years*, p. 372; Cottle received Wordsworth's letter of 12 April 'soon after'). On this occasion Wordsworth read to Cottle 'many of his Lyrical Pieces, when I immediately perceived in them extraordinary merit, and advised him to publish them.... To the idea of publishing he expressed a strong objection, and after several interviews, I left him, with an earnest wish that he would reconsider his determination.' Since Cottle was offered Wordsworth's poems in mid-March (*C.L.*, i. 399–400), (*a*) Cottle's visit was earlier than late March and Coleridge's letter reports Wordsworth's reconsideration; or (*b*) Cottle is reporting, not quite accurately, Wordsworth's reluctance to publish his shorter poems without Coleridge's (*C.L.*, i. 411–12); or (*c*) Wordsworth was more anxious to publish his longer poems than his 'Lyrical Pieces'; or (*d*) Cottle is merely confused.

'volume of Poems', comprising 'Salisbury Plain & Tale of a Woman . . . with a few others', is, however, still available to Cottle at thirty guineas (*C.L.*, i. 402). At the end of April, Dorothy informs Richard Wordsworth that William 'is about to publish some poems. He is to have twenty guineas for one volume, and he expects more than twice as much for another which is nearly ready for publishing' (*E.Y.*, p. 216).[1] During April, it appears, Wordsworth's stock of poems, as distinct from *The Borderers*, has grown from one volume to two, and Cottle has made offers for them. The potential contents of these volumes is uncertain: Mrs. Moorman suggests 'Wordsworth's long poems, *Salisbury Plain* and *Peter Bell*, in one volume, and the shorter poems in another' (*Early Years*, p. 372).[2] In late May or early June this proposal, or something very similar, was rejected: 'W. would not object to the publishing of Peter Bell *or* the Salisbury Plain, singly; but to the publishing of *his poems* in two volumes he is decisively repugnant & oppugnant—He deems that they would want variety &c &c—if this apply in his case, it applies with tenfold force to mine.—We deem that the volumes offered to you are to a certain degree *one work*, in *kind tho' not in degree*, as an Ode is one work—& that our different poems are as stanzas, good relatively rather than

---

[1] The source of this information does not seem to appear in any published document. It perhaps derives from a reply from Cottle to Coleridge's letter dated 'Early April' by Griggs (*C.L.*, i. 402).

[2] *Salisbury Plain* was still to be finished on 9 May, and Cottle, Wordsworth is determined, will publish it (*E.Y.*, p. 218). Cottle (*Reminiscences*, pp. 134–5) says that he spent a week at Alfoxden as a result of the invitations contained in Wordsworth's letter of 9 May and Coleridge's of uncertain date (*C.L.*, i. 403); that he heard poems read and visited Lynmouth, Lynton, and the Valley of Stones; and that the publication of *Lyrical Ballads* was arranged during this visit. Is this tour to Lynmouth, &c. (which must, however, have been in late May rather than in the spring) the source of Wordsworth's confusion in the I.F. note to *We are Seven*?

absolutely' (*C.L.*, i. 411–12). The implications of this passage and its context seem to be: (1) Cottle has offered to publish all Wordsworth's available poems (except *The Borderers* and, probably, *The Ruined Cottage*) in two volumes; and (2) he has also offered to publish Coleridge's poems, including *Osorio*, which is referred to in depreciatory terms a little later in Coleridge's letter. (3) Wordsworth will consider the publication of *Salisbury Plain* or *Peter Bell* as a separate volume; but (4) he does not wish to publish a second volume containing only his smaller poems. (5) On the contrary, he and Coleridge insist that any publication of Wordsworth's shorter poems shall be together with Coleridge's, and that *Osorio* shall be represented only by extracts. (6) They insist on this course because they agree that each poet's works published separately 'would want variety'—or, as Wordsworth put it in the Preface of 1800: 'For the sake of variety and from a consciousness of my own weakness I was induced to request the assistance of a Friend, who furnished me with [several poems]. I should not, however, have requested this assistance, had I not believed that the poems of my Friend would in a great measure have the same tendency as my own, and that, though there would be found a difference, there would be found no discordance in the colours of our style. . . .' Why Coleridge writes of the 'volumes' (rather than 'volume') offered to Cottle is not quite clear: either he thinks still of one volume comprising a large work or works by Wordsworth, plus a joint volume of smaller poems; or he thinks of the joint poems which were shortly to become *Lyrical Ballads* as extending over two volumes.[1]

[1] The second explanation is in accord with Cottle, *Reminiscences*, p. 135: 'I had recommended two volumes, but one was fixed on. . . . A day or two after [these arrangements were made] I received [Coleridge's letter of ?28 May, *C.L.*, i. 411]'. *Lyrical Ballads*, 1798, would have spread very thinly over two volumes, and it may be that Cottle's

INTRODUCTION

Of all the contemporary documents, only the letter of Coleridge to Cottle last cited contains any hint of the concept of large-scale artistic collaboration which both Wordsworth and Coleridge in later years presented as the germ of *Lyrical Ballads*. True, Dorothy Wordsworth's letter of 20 November 1797 speaks of joint planning of *The Ancient Mariner*, and the I.F. note to *We are Seven* of an attempt 'to proceed conjointly' with the poem which does not, however, seem to have lasted longer than the evening of 13 November. Wordsworth goes on, in terms reminiscent of the opening of *Biographia Literaria*, Chapter XIV, and of his own Preface of 1802, to mention 'talk of a Volume which was to consist, as Mr. Coleridge has told the world, of Poems chiefly on supernatural subjects [and subjects] taken from common life but looked at, as much as might be, through an imaginative medium'. Coleridge implies (*Biog. Lit.*, ii. 5) that Wordsworth's poems of the spring and early summer of 1798 had their philosophic origin in conversations between the poets 'During the first year that Mr. Wordsworth and I were neighbours', that is, in 1797;[1] the facts do not contradict this, but only the suggestion, especially noticeable in Coleridge's account, that the experimental poems, as well as his own on supernatural themes, were the final fruit of a long and purposeful series of discussions on poetics beginning some time in 1797 and reaching practice in the period November 1797–summer 1798. No doubt there were such discussions, and they may have borne a harvest beginning in March 1798; but it was a harvest curiously postponed by Wordsworth's concern with *The Borderers* and with narrative and meditative blank

---

'recommendation' was inferred from Coleridge's letter, which was talking about the possible publication of all Wordsworth's available poems in two volumes.

[1] More strictly summer 1797–summer 1798.

verse of a kind rarely represented in his contributions to *Lyrical Ballads*. The suggestion (*Biog. Lit.*, ii. 5–6) of a well planned 'series of poems', on two types of subject, with the labour neatly divided between the two authors, is a little too rational for the facts. Of Coleridge's contributions to the book, only *The Ancient Mariner* (as he admits, *Biog. Lit.*, ii. 6) bears any relation to such a series; and no poems of Wordsworth's which are known to have been conceived contemporaneously with *The Ancient Mariner* appear in *Lyrical Ballads*. In other words, if we believe Coleridge's account in *Biographia Literaria*, we must suppose either that Wordsworth postponed his share of the planned series for some four months (from the pressure of other work or from mere lack of inspiration), or that the plan of the series was an *ex post facto* one devised when *The Ancient Mariner* was wholly or partly finished. Moreover, the joint publication is presented by Coleridge, paradoxically (or typically, in view of his characteristic thinking in terms of the reconciliation of opposites), both as 'to a certain degree *one work*' and as a tribute to the need for 'variety' (*C.L.*, i. 412)—a paradox which is more or less followed by Wordsworth in the Preface of 1800. The fact is, as Reed shows, that from March 1798, in spite of the importance of Coleridge's contributions, the dominant personality behind *Lyrical Ballads* is Wordsworth's: for the theory of the Advertisement and Preface is basically his, and draws attention to his own rather than to Coleridge's contributions; he was even anxious to drop *The Ancient Mariner* from the edition of 1800 (*E.Y.*, pp. 263–4), and, when it was retained, wrote an obtuse note exposing its alleged defects.

By the end of May 1798 it is clear that Cottle has accepted for publication the joint volume which would eventually be called *Lyrical Ballads*: 'William has now some poems in the

Bristol press... William has sold his poems very advantageously' (*E.Y.*, p. 219; 31 May 1798). The record proceeds: 'William's poems are now in the press; they will be out in six weeks' (*E.Y.*, p. 226; 18 July 1798); '[William's poems are] printed, but not published. [They are] in one small volume, without the name of the author; their title is "Lyrical Ballads, with other Poems". Cottle has given thirty guineas for William's share of the volume' (*E.Y.*, p. 227; 13 September 1798). In a letter of May 1799, Wordsworth writes to Cottle: 'The day before I left England [15 September 1798] I wrote to you to request that you would transfer your right to the *Lyrical Ballads* to Mr. Johnson, on account of its being likely to be very advantageous to me... I had not time to receive your answer so I do not know how the poems have been disposed of. Pray let me hear from you immediately' (*E.Y.*, p. 259). By 2 June he had received a reply, stating that Cottle had not been able to follow Wordsworth's instruction because he had already transferred the edition to J. & A. Arch (*E.Y.*, p. 262; Cottle, *Reminiscences*, pp. 193-4). The book was advertised as published by Arch on 4 October 1798; and by Arch's name hangs the tale of further obscurity in the progress of *Lyrical Ballads* towards publication.

II

While the name 'J. & A. Arch' figures on the title-page of most copies of *Lyrical Ballads*, 1798, certain copies[1] bear the imprint: 'Bristol: Printed by Biggs and Cottle, For T. N. Longman, Paternoster-row, London.' Moreover, the contents of the book varies from copy to copy within certain limits. The bibliographical evidence for this state of affairs, brilliantly set forth and explained by D. F. Foxon,[2] is too complex for

[1] Thirteen known copies are recorded by Healey, item 3.
[2] 'The Printing of *Lyrical Ballads*, 1798', *The Library*, 5th series, ix (1954), 221-41.

the scope of this introduction; but a summary of the facts and of Foxon's conclusions is possible.

It is clear that it was at first intended to issue *Lyrical Ballads* with Coleridge's *Lewti*[1] in the place now occupied by his *The Nightingale*; copies exist so arranged and with a Table of Contents which reads accordingly. It is also clear that the final intention was to issue the book with *The Nightingale* substituted for *Lewti*; and to make this change a four-leaf cancel (paged [63], 64–69, [70]) was substituted for leaves D8, E1–2 (pp. 63–68) of the original printing. Since the cancel contained one leaf (two pages) more than what it replaced, the book in its final form is paged [63]–69, [70], [69]–70, &c., though, because of the omission of page-numbers from a blank page and a page with a dropped title-line, no page-number is actually printed twice. At least one copy, formerly belonging to Robert Southey, exists in which these two states are combined: *Lewti* is in its original place before *The Female Vagrant*, but *The Nightingale* also appears after the *Yew-tree* lines, and the book contains a Contents page listing *Lewti*. It is commonly supposed that it was decided to cancel *Lewti* because it had already been published, over the *nom de plume* 'Nicias Erythraeus', in *The Morning Post* for 13 April 1798 and was known to be Coleridge's; thus the anonymity of the authors[2] would have been destroyed by its republication. One other state of the book is recorded: it contains *The Nightingale*, but also, on an inserted leaf numbered 62★ and 63★,[3] a poem called *Domiciliary Verses, December, 1795*, by Dr. Thomas

---

[1] A reworking of an early poem by Wordsworth called *Beauty and Moonlight*; see *W.P.W.*, i. 263–4, and *C.P.W.*, i. 253–6, ii. 1049–52.

[2] Defended by Coleridge in his letter to Cottle of ?28 May 1798, on the ground that 'Wordsworth's name is nothing—to a large number of persons mine *stinks*' (*C.L.*, i. 412).

[3] Recto and verso respectively; but a recto page should have an odd page-number.

Beddoes, father of the poet T. L. Beddoes. It is supposed that this poem was the first to be substituted for *Lewti*, and that it was subsequently replaced by *The Nightingale*.[1]

One other curiosity must be mentioned: on 5 September Southey wrote to his friend William Taylor of Norwich: 'Have you seen a volume of *Lyrical Ballads*, etc.? They are by Coleridge and Wordsworth, but their names are not affixed'; and he goes on to criticize the work, especially *The Ancient Mariner*, in phrases which reappear in his review of the book in the *Critical Review*. Since, according to Dorothy Wordsworth's letter of 13 September, *Lyrical Ballads* was then 'printed, but not published', Southey must have gained his information from proof-sheets or advance copies; he must also have been ignorant of the fact that the book was unpublished on 5 September (and indeed on 13 September), since he assumes that Taylor may have seen a (published) copy.

Several questions arise: (1) Why did Cottle not publish the book himself, after all the correspondence, cited earlier, which looks forward to such a publication?[2] (2) Was the book ever published by Longman, as the Bristol title-page implies? If so, why did *Cottle* transfer the edition to Arch, and if not, why not? (3) Why did Cottle transfer the edition to Arch at such a date that the book was unpublished on 13 September, but that he could not follow Wordsworth's instruction of 15 September (which must have reached him about 17 September) to transfer it to Johnson?

Cottle himself claimed that he transferred the edition to

---

[1] Foxon, p. 233, suggests that this copy was for presentation to Dr. Beddoes, who had presumably given permission for his poem to be used and would expect to see it in a printed copy of the book.

[2] Foxon, p. 240, points out that the normal form of imprint for books published by Cottle is 'printed by Biggs & Cottle and sold by T. N. Longman', not '. . . for T. N. Longman', which implies publication by Longman.

INTRODUCTION

Arch 'at a loss' because of the 'heavy' (i.e., slow, sluggish) sale of the book;[1] but since the book was unpublished on 13 September and transferred to Arch by about 17 September, Cottle could hardly have had time to assess its sale, and the motive for the transfer which he assigns is thus not very credible. Thomas Hutchinson proposed that Southey warned Cottle that the book was unlikely to sell and that he should get rid of it to avoid loss; this, as Foxon shows, is possible, but not in the sense Hutchinson intended; moreover, Hutchinson's account is based on the false assumption that the book was published in Bristol by about 1 September.[2]

The sequence of events suggested by Foxon seems much more credible: that Cottle originally intended to publish the book himself, and may even have printed an appropriate title-page; but that, either because he had been warned against this course by Southey or for some other, unexplained reason, he negotiated, or hoped to negotiate, with Longman for the publication. He printed a title-page in accordance with these negotiations or hopes, and made up copies of the book containing it for the authors and his friends and theirs. Thus copies with the Bristol title-page were not published, but advance copies[3] prepared in anticipation of publication by Longman. The negotiations, Foxon suggests, came to nothing; so that in mid-September, as Dorothy Wordsworth indicates, the book was 'printed, but not published'. It was not published because, at that date, no publisher had been found; but almost immediately and simultaneously two were

---

[1] Cottle, *Reminiscences*, p. 194. He claims (p. 139) that the book was published 'about Midsummer, 1798'.

[2] Hutchinson, pp. ix, xvi.

[3] 'Since Cottle had a large circle of friends in Bristol, and since Wordsworth and Coleridge presumably wanted a number of copies, it would not be difficult to visualize some twenty-five copies circulating in this way, of which some twelve are known' (Foxon, p. 239).

found, Arch by Cottle and Johnson by Wordsworth, then in London preparing to leave for Germany. Cottle agreed with Arch before he received Wordsworth's instructions to transfer the book to Johnson; he printed a new title-page, and the book was accordingly published by Arch on 4 October 1798.

III

Utilitarian motives for publication and an over-rationalized account of philosophical origins are not a very promising background for a book of 'new' poetry; yet the fact remains that *Lyrical Ballads* is a highly significant book in the development of the authors (especially of Wordsworth) and in the history of English literature. Like many such books, it is at once novel and traditional, echoing the past in themes and forms while it uses them for new purposes or new emphases or new insights.

To the modern reader, the most obviously traditional poem in the book is, no doubt, *The Ancient Mariner*, modelled, as the Advertisement states, on 'the *style*, as well as . . . the spirit of the elder poets'. It is in fact a narrative ballad, modelled more or less on the traditional ballad which Coleridge would have known from Thomas Percy's collection *Reliques of Ancient English Poetry* (1765), and on other types, including German literary ballads such as the famous *Lenore* of Bürger, translated several times in the nineties and freely reprinted in magazines. My phrase is 'modelled more or less' since Coleridge's masterpiece differs, in the direction of 'literature', from the typical traditional ballad for which the modern reader would turn to the standard *English and Scottish Popular Ballads* of F. J. Child.[1] While the poem uses, obviously, the metre of the ballad and a quasi-archaic diction for which Coleridge went to many sources from Chaucer to the

[1] Boston, 1882–98.

voyagers of the seventeenth and eighteenth centuries, and while it employs some of the rhetorical devices of the traditional ballad, it is nevertheless too long, too diffuse, and too complex to be a wholly convincing imitation of a traditional ballad. The sources of Coleridge's plot, imagery, and diction are sketched in my notes; the obvious rhetorical device which Coleridge learned from traditional ballads is significant repetition, and in particular what is commonly called 'incremental repetition', whereby partial repetition of image or phrase is accompanied by a new motif which adds an 'increment' of narrative fact at each repetition. Thus ll. 13 and 17 add information while they repeat the general sense of l. 9:

> But still he holds the wedding-guest . . .
> He holds him with his skinny hand . . .
> He holds him with his glittering eye . . .

Of the following stanzas, the second repeats, with negatives foreboding the tragedy of the poem, the drift of the first:

> And a good south wind sprung up behind,
>   The Albatross did follow;
> And every day for food or play
>   Came to the Marinere's hollo . . .
> And the good south wind still blew behind,
>   But no sweet Bird did follow
> Ne any day for food or play
>   Came to the Marinere's hollo! (69–72, 85–88)

The ignorant folly of the crew is conveyed in this repetition:

> . . . all averr'd, I had kill'd the Bird
>   That made the Breeze to blow . . .
> Then all averr'd, I had kill'd the Bird
>   That brought the fog and mist . . . (91–92, 95–96)

The next two stanzas, by their repetition, emphasize the progress of the narrative and of the damnation of the crew;

and the challenge of discovery is replaced in a moment by the despair of the desert:

> The breezes blew, the white foam flew,
>   The furrow follow'd free:
> We were the first that ever burst
>   Into that silent Sea.
>
> Down dropt the breeze, the Sails dropt down,
>   'Twas sad as sad could be
> And we did speak only to break
>   The silence of the Sea. (99–106)

In passages such as these Coleridge achieves something of the 'flint and iron' quality of the traditional ballad.

This quality, or rather the means by which it is sometimes conveyed—the plain factual statement of event after event, without emphasis on any particular event at the expense of any other—is used by Coleridge for another purpose: to secure what he called, in a famous phrase, a 'willing suspension of disbelief' in the supernatural events of the poem.[1] Because the earlier and more easily credible stages of the Mariner's voyage are presented in this way, the reader all the more readily accepts, as another in the chain of credible events which do not need to be questioned, such a happening as the approach of the spectral ship in Part III of the poem.

The Ancient Mariner lacks—to its disadvantage, not as a narrative poem, but as an imitation of the traditional ballad—the quality which Thomas Gray found in *Child Maurice*: 'It begins in the fifth act of the play'.[2] This quality of spareness, or under-statement, or minimal statement, which in the best ballads gives the impression of intense concentration by the poet on the barest essentials of the plot, and which in poor or

---

[1] *Biog. Lit.*, ii. 6.
[2] Gray to Mason, June 1757; *Correspondence*, ed. Toynbee and Whibley (Oxford, 1935), p. 505.

INTRODUCTION xxiii

poorly preserved ballads often leads to mere obscurity, is on the whole sacrificed by Coleridge, and by other imitators of ballads in this age, in favour of a comparatively complex and complete narrative. We infer details—'The Sun came up upon the left' (29), so that the ship must have been sailing south—but we are not asked, as a ballad like *Child Maurice* demands, to infer a whole series of family relations between the characters, or to guess, as *Sir Patrick Spens* makes us guess, why Sir Patrick was ordered by his king to undertake a disastrous voyage in dangerous weather.

In this respect Coleridge diverges from his models in the direction of fullness, ease of comprehension, and a general spaciousness with which the lavish imagery of the poem, gathered from his wide reading, is congruous. Neither method of writing a ballad is necessarily preferable: what emerges is the difference between the model, or the tradition, which is Coleridge's literary basis, and the new poem. We shall be concerned to trace comparable divergences in other kinds of poem contained in *Lyrical Ballads*.

One such divergence can be seen in Coleridge's *The Nightingale* and Wordsworth's *Yew-tree* lines and the poem commonly called *Tintern Abbey*.[1] The meditative poem in blank verse, frequently concerned with the natural scene and the philosophical inferences of the poet from what he sees and hears, had something like a century of tradition to its name when Wordsworth came to handle it in the nineties. Derived ultimately from the blank verse of Milton's *Paradise Lost*, it descends to the Romantic poets through the parody and imitation of John Philips[2] and more especially through

[1] Although the poem has nothing to do with Tintern Abbey, it was so called by Wordsworth at least as early as 1809 (*M.Y.*, p. 308).
[2] *The Splendid Shilling* (1701), *Cerealia* (1706), *Cyder* (1708); and others.

such poems as James Thomson's *The Seasons* (1726-30), Mark Akenside's *Pleasures of Imagination* (1744), and William Cowper's *The Task* (1785). What is new in Wordsworth's handling of this kind of poem? Not, on the whole, the precision of the natural description, unless in the consistency of Wordsworth's success: Thomson and Cowper provide many instances of equally fine observation as adequately reported. Consider, however, a well-known passage in this manner from *The Prelude* (VI. 624-40):

> The immeasurable height
> Of woods decaying, never to be decayed,
> The stationary blasts of waterfalls,
> And in the narrow rent at every turn
> Winds thwarting winds, bewildered and forlorn,
> The torrents shooting from the clear blue sky,
> The rocks that muttered close upon our ears,
> Black drizzling crags that spake by the way-side
> As if a voice were in them, the sick sight
> And giddy prospect of the raving stream,
> The unfettered clouds and region of the Heavens,
> Tumult and peace, the darkness and the light—
> Were all like workings of one mind, the features
> Of the same face, blossoms upon one tree;
> Characters of the great Apocalypse,
> The types and symbols of Eternity,
> Of first, and last, and midst, and without end.

What is remarkable about this description is the homogeneous nature of the images and the use to which this homogeneity is put. Almost all involve, in some way or other, the concept which the physicist would call energy: energy constantly expended ('woods decaying . . . blasts of waterfalls . . . Winds thwarting winds . . . torrents shooting . . . rocks that muttered . . . crags that spake') but never exhausted ('never to be decayed ... stationary blasts ... at every turn'). The paradox of energy always expended and always renewed suggests to Wordsworth that these images are 'types and symbols of Eternity': eternity, if it could be made palpable, might consist in just that. In such a passage, qualities inherent in natural objects are seen to be, also, embodiments of a philosophical abstraction. We shall recognize the advance in poetic insight in such a passage if we compare it with Thomson's description of the 'Thrice happy man' who seeks out shade in the heat of summer and

> Sits coolly calm; while all the world without,
> Unsatisfied and sick, tosses in noon.
> Emblem instructive of the virtuous man,
> Who keeps his tempered mind serene and pure,
> And every passion aptly harmonized
> Amid a jarring world with vice inflamed.
>
> (*Summer*, 463–8)

The literal coolness of the happy man is an emblem of virtue only because of a kind of pun on the word (or notion of) *heat* used literally, in the preceding description, and metaphorically ('with vice inflamed'). The metaphor is long dead, and the heat of summer no longer strikes as a vivid 'emblem' for vice. In Wordsworth's lines, the quality of the natural objects as he describes them is as inherent as it is in his concept of eternity. There is an inevitability in this symbolism which is lacking in Thomson's emblem.

What is comparable in, say, *Tintern Abbey*? What philosophical abstraction emerges from this poem of natural description and biographical summary? A concept more difficult to define, perhaps: a continuity in human experience of nature. The poet's own experience of nature is traced, in its relevance to his reaction to this scene on the Wye, from boyhood to his present mood of 'sad perplexity' mingled with 'pleasing thoughts' (61 ff.). To this continuous experience of nature he now adds his sister's, and recognizes, in her voice and eyes, a recurrence, or repetition, of his own 'former pleasures' in her reaction to the scene; whence he infers a continuity of his experience in hers. The landscape itself echoes or typifies this: it is connected 'with the quiet of the sky' (7–8), as if land and sky were one; the greenness of summer provides a continuity of colour (11–15, 18); the hedgerows are continuous with the wood (16–17). The physical continuities so described act as a kind of emblem of the poet's experience which is being described.

IV

The traditionalism of other Wordsworthian poems is more difficult to trace because its origins are in verse which has not the literary quality nor, consequently, the reputation of the forbears of *Tintern Abbey*. But in recent years analogues to various Wordsworthian poems of seemingly original form and theme have been found in the poetry sections of the magazines of the nineties,[1] to one of which, we remember, Wordsworth and Coleridge had once considered offering *The Ancient Mariner*. One such poetic kind is the brief lyric (as distinct from the comparatively long blank-verse poem) dealing with the natural scene and the poet's reaction to it or meditation upon it. Such are *Lines written at a small Distance . . .*,[2] *Lines written*

[1] Robert Mayo, 'The Contemporaneity of the "Lyrical Ballads"', *P.M.L.A.*, lxix (1954), 486–522.

[2] Mayo points out that long titles of this kind (represented also by the full titles of the *Yew-tree* lines and *Tintern Abbey*) are common in the magazines: *Address to the Nightingale, on first hearing her in a Walk in the Fields in the Night of April 25, 1790; Address to the Nightingale on hearing her in a Tree adjoining a Church-yard; Verses, written at an antient Abbey of Nuns, now gone to Decay* (*Gentleman's*, June and October 1790; February 1791).

in early Spring, and the companion pieces *Expostulation and Reply* and *The Tables Turned*.

The tone of such pieces may be seen from the following irregular sonnet, *The Prospect of Spring* by W. Hamilton Reid, which was thought worthy of publication by at least two magazines (*Scots*, February 1790; *European*, February 1790):

> The Snow-drop marks the early tints of Spring,
> And soon the plumy heralds of the year,
> Nestling, shall speak the cheerful season near,
> And social melodies in concert sing.
> Again, with genial glow the nymphs shall charm,
> The whisp'ring groves with leafy green be hung;
> Love's potent influence youthful bosoms 'larm,
> And soft persuasion dwell upon each tongue;
> And the broad table of the foodful earth
> Recruit the sinews of laborious toil;
> And Hope, and Pleasure, and light-footed Mirth
> Beat tuneful rapture to th'increasing smile
> Of Earth and Heav'n—and summer scenes ensue,
> In all the beauties of the sunny hue.

Or the following lyric ('by Mrs. Darwall'), *On hearing a Blackbird sing early in March* (*Scots*, October 1795):[1]

> Welcome sweet harbinger of Spring!
> Thou softest warbler of the grove!
> Thou bid'st the dreary woodlands ring
> With strains of music, joy and love.
>
> Tho' scarce a swelling bud is seen
> To deck the hedge-row, shrub or tree;
> Tho' Nature boasts no vivid green,
> Yet is gay Spring announc'd by thee.

[1] The tone is also similar to that of the comparatively numerous poems (mainly written in 1802, published in 1807, and later included in the class 'Poems of the Fancy') in which Wordsworth addresses small birds and common flowers.

> When, rising from th'unblossom'd spray,
> Thy sooty fav'rite meets thine eye,
> How quick thou wing'st thy liquid way,
> Regardless of the stormy sky!
>
> True love, and well-try'd faith, can bear,
> Unmov'd, the chilling wintry blast,
> Sing o'er the scanty hard-earn'd fare,
> Nor e'er regret the sunshine past.

The poets dwell upon the natural scene with as much fidelity as the stilted diction (especially that of the first poem)[1] will permit; they are in that condition which Wordsworth describes in *Tintern Abbey* as outmoded in his own experience: subject to 'a feeling and a love, That had no need of a remoter charm, By thought supplied'. In Wordsworth's *Lines written in early Spring*, the natural scene is used primarily as a stimulus for the 'thought' which was lacking in his experience of nature in 1793: curious meditation on the possibility 'that every flower Enjoys the air it breathes' and that natural processes in plants and birds subsist through what the Preface of 1802 calls 'the grand elementary principle of pleasure'. *Expostulation and Reply* and *The Tables Turned* expound the educative value of the mere experience of the natural scene, and contrast it with the merely rational gains—if gains they are—accruing from book-learning.

More important than these poems (or so Wordsworth's theoretical discussions would suggest) are those to which he obviously referred when he wrote of 'experiments' in Advertisement and Preface. The fact is that the forms and themes of the most characteristic *Lyrical Ballads* are less original that Wordsworth's prose suggests: the magazines abound in

[1] Note 'plumy heralds of the year ... genial glow ... nymphs ... whisp'ring groves ... youthful bosoms ... laborious toil'; 'warbler of the grove ... sooty fav'rite'.

INTRODUCTION   xxix

poems, in ballad-stanzas, ballad-like stanzas, and in other forms, about the poor, the misguided, the abandoned, and even the criminal and the insane, such as figure largely in Wordsworth's contributions to the book.

Thus in the *Gentleman's Magazine* for September 1791 we find a poem, in the stanza of Gray's *Elegy*, entitled *The Beggar's Petition*. Like the Old Cumberland Beggar from whom Wordsworth developed the figure of his Old Man Travelling, the beggar is a 'poor old man, Whose trembling limbs have borne him to your door'. Like the heroine's father in *The Female Vagrant*, he inherited 'a little farm'; but 'Oppression forc'd me from my cot'; and, more or less like the Vagrant herself,

> My daughter, once the comfort of my age,
> Lur'd by a villain from her native home,
> Is cast, abandoned, on the world's wide stage,
> And doom'd in scanty poverty to roam.

The *Gentleman's* for September 1798 contains *The Beggar Boy* (in four eight-line stanzas, like Wordsworth's in *Goody Blake* and *Simon Lee*); the *European* for November 1792 contains an *Elegy. The Dead Beggar. Written in the Churchyard at Brighthelmston, on seeing the Funeral of a Pauper who perished for Want* . . . By Charlotte Smith.

The convicted criminal, the subject of Wordsworth's *The Convict*, is also the subject of *On the Necessity of Solitary Confinement, The Complaint of a Transport in Botany Bay, The Condemned Criminal's Soliloquy; said to have been found in the Cell of the Unfortunate Griffiths, alias Hubbard, alias Lord Massey, after his Execution, A Prison*, and *On reading Mr. Howard's Account of Lazarettos, from Poems by the Rev. W. L. Bowles, A. M.* (*Gentleman's*, March and June 1792, February 1793, September 1798; *Annual Register*, 1794). Deserted mothers or lovers appear, as in Wordsworth's *The Thorn* and *The Mad Mother*, in *Edwin and Colla* (*Gentleman's*, July 1798), *The Lass of Fair Wone* (*Scots*, July 1796; a possible source for *The Thorn*), and in *Malvina, A Dirge* (*Scots*, June 1798); madness, as in *The Thorn*, *The Mad Mother*, and *The Idiot Boy*, in *Malvina*, just cited, and *Ellen; or, The Fair Insane* (*Scots*, February 1795). Thomas Lister contributes a sentimental blank verse piece *The Prostitute* to *Gentleman's*, July 1798.

Here, clearly, is a collection of themes entirely comparable to Wordsworth's in his treatment, in the experimental poems of *Lyrical Ballads*, of the unfortunates, the outcasts, or the abnormal members of society. We seek, again, a distinction between such verse and Wordsworth's; and we find it, again, in a superiority of insight, in a deeper understanding of the subject than is usually to be found in the contributors to the magazines. One emotion is commonly played upon by the magazine poets in such verse as is instanced above: it is pity. 'Pity the sorrows of a poor old man', begins *The Beggar's Petition* (*Gentleman's*, September 1791). The convict in Bowles's *On reading Mr. Howard's Account* is thus described:

> Cold is his frozen heart—his eye is rear'd
> To Heaven no more—and on his sable beard
> The tear has ceas'd to fall. Thou canst not bring
> Back to his mournful heart the morn of spring.
> Thou canst not bid the rose of health renew,
> Upon his wasted cheek her crimson hue.

From this kind of sentimentality Wordsworth's own early *The Convict* is not free; but the poems of 1798 do not, on the whole, work on the reader in this way. Wordsworth is not concerned to pity so much as to understand:[1] he is concerned,

[1] In *Prel.*, XIII. 221 ff., Wordsworth reports a prophecy which he made, after he had passed his 'crisis' and recovered his 'Imagination and Taste', on the subject-matter of his verse: it includes 'Sorrow, that is not

INTRODUCTION xxxi

as he put it in the Preface of 1800, 'to follow the fluxes and refluxes of the mind when agitated by the great and simple affections of our nature', or to provide, as he stated in his note to *The Thorn* of the same date, a 'history or science of feelings'. The poems are, in fact, concerned to trace the persistence of essentially normal states of mind in situations of emotional stress or even of mental derangement. It is as if Wordsworth wished to affirm, or even to celebrate, the dominance of the normal human spirit in circumstances in which its breakdown might perhaps be expected. He traces, as the Preface says, 'the maternal passion through many of its more subtle windings, as in the poems of the IDIOT BOY and the MAD MOTHER'; that is, he shows that a mother's love for her child survives even the idiocy of the child and the madness of the mother. He examines attitudes to death in the *Forsaken Indian* and *We are Seven*: that of the dying and that of the child so much alive that death has no meaning. A poem such as *The Last of the Flock*, while it may call forth the reader's pity, is also concerned to display the validity of a man's feeling for hard-won property when that feeling is in actual or potential conflict with his affection for his family. The possible effect of a curse upon the physical organism of man is demonstrated in *Goody Blake*, whether we say, as Wordsworth does in his Preface, that 'the power of the human imagination' brings about the effect; or whether we fall into modern jargon and call it auto-suggestion; or whether, assuming the 'willing suspension of disbelief' of which Coleridge writes, we merely suppose that curses *per se* are effective: given the circumstances, the mind works like that, dictating bodily

sorrow, but delight; And miserable love, that is not pain To hear of'. In the Preface of 1802 he claims that 'more pathetic situations and sentiments, that is, those which have a greater proportion of pain connected with them, may be endured in metrical composition, especially in rhyme, than in prose'.

sensation. *The Thorn*, if we accept Wordsworth's account of his purpose, displays a superstitious mind playing upon rumour and on observed but not fully connected facts, fascinated in spite of, or perhaps because of, the undecipherable truth of the whole situation of Martha Ray.[1]

Why was Wordsworth so intent upon tracing the persistence of more or less normal psychic processes in more or less abnormal psychic situations? The Preface of 1800 tells us, in a not very satisfactory argument,[2] why he chose situations in 'Low and rustic life' for the purpose, but not what suggested the purpose. The answer to that question is provided by *The Prelude* and other comment on Wordsworth's intellectual progress in the nineties. He had accepted the French Revolution as a natural and necessary event, at least to the point of the execution of the king. Subsequent excesses turned him against it, and especially his observation of the perversion of normal psychic processes in such contexts as those of the September Massacres and the Terror. 'The study of human nature', he wrote in a prefatory note to *The Borderers*,

suggests this awful truth, that, as . . . sin and crime are apt to start from their very opposite qualities, so are there no limits to the hardening of the heart, and the perversion of the understanding to which they may carry their slaves. During my long residence in France, while the revolution was rapidly advancing to its extreme of

[1] The critics (including Coleridge) who persist in reading *The Thorn* as a badly-told tale of a deserted unmarried mother who murdered her child miss, amongst others, the point of the narrator's uncertainty whether 'a child was born or no', whether ' 'twas born alive or dead', and whether Martha Ray murdered it if it was born alive (ll. 159, 161, 223-4): this uncertainty resembles the uneasiness of the mind faced with what it thinks is, or may be, supernatural. For a subtle reading of the poem, see John F. Danby, *The Simple Wordsworth* (London, 1960), pp. 57-72.

[2] See the discussion in W. J. B. Owen, *Wordsworth's Preface to* Lyrical Ballads (Copenhagen, 1957), pp. 14-21.

wickedness, I had frequent opportunities of being an eye-witness of this process. (*W.P.W.*, i. 342)

The 'truth' is demonstrated in the play itself, and is further discussed in its prefatory essay which Wordsworth did not publish (*W.P.W.*, i. 345–9). He was put under considerable distress by the entry of Britain into the war against France (11 February 1793), and even more by the aggressive activities of France in Europe from perhaps 1794 onward. He was, he indicates in *The Prelude*, under the influence of, or at least interested in, the rationalizing theories of William Godwin's *Political Justice*, as a result of these distresses, and is known to have been in comparatively frequent personal contact with Godwin in 1795 (*Prel.*, X. 263 ff., XI. 173 ff., 206 ff., 223 ff.; Moorman, *Early Years*, pp. 262 ff.). Whatever his precise indebtedness to Godwin, it is clear that, by the time he wrote *The Prelude*, Wordsworth saw himself as pursuing, in the middle nineties, a course of thinking which paid too much attention to merely rational processes. He thought he saw man's improvement achieved 'by such means As did not lie in nature' (*Prel.* [1805], X. 843–4);[1] he thought he learned something of truth by the process, but also

> errors into which I was betray'd
> By present objects, and by reasoning false
> From the beginning, inasmuch as drawn
> Out of a heart which had been turn'd aside
> From nature by external accidents,
> And which was thus confounded more and more,
> Misguiding and misguided. Thus I fared,
> Dragging all passions, notions, shapes of faith,
> Like culprits to the bar, suspiciously
> Calling the mind to establish in plain day

[1] The sense of *nature* here and in the next quotation is probably 'normal human behaviour', 'the norm of human behaviour'.

> Her titles and her honours, now believing,
> Now disbelieving, endlessly perplex'd
> With impulse, motive, right and wrong, the ground
> Of moral obligation, what the rule
> And what the sanction, till, demanding *proof*,
> And seeking it in everything, I lost
> All feeling of conviction, and, in fine,
> Sick, wearied out with contrarieties,
> Yielded up moral questions in despair.
>
> (*Prel.* [1805], X. 883–901)

At this point, he says, he turned from the attempt to rationalize human behaviour to the study of mathematics, where the reason had its proper field of activity: as he put it in *The Prelude*, he

> turned to abstract science, and there sought
> Work for the reasoning faculty enthroned
> Where the disturbances of space and time—
> Whether in matters various, properties
> Inherent, or from human will and power
> Derived—find no admission. (XI. 328–33)

From this sterile occupation he was drawn towards what he earlier called 'The exactness of a comprehensive mind' (*Prel.* [1805], X. 845), or to 'nature', by the restorative influence of his sister (*Prel.*, XI. 335 ff.). He abandoned, he says, a merely intellectual approach to the external natural scene (*Prel.*, XII. 88 ff.); he 'found Once more in Man an object of delight' (XIII. 48–49); he saw through political and economic theorizings (XIII. 64–79) and gained

> A more judicious knowledge of the worth
> And dignity of individual man,
> No composition of the brain, but man
> Of whom we read, the man whom we behold
> With our own eyes; (XIII. 80–84)

and he proceeded to study man where, he supposed, he could best be found in his unsophisticated state, 'Among the natural abodes of men, Fields with their rural works' (XIII. 102–3):[1] in other words, in the 'Low and rustic life' which, says the Preface of 1800, was to provide the subject-matter of the experimental poems of *Lyrical Ballads*.

In sum: Wordsworth celebrated the normal in mankind in *Lyrical Ballads* because, having trusted 'nature', the normal, in his youth, and having been led by 'overpressure from the times And their disastrous issues' (*Prel.*, XII. 51–52) to mistrust the normal, he had had his faith in it restored to such a degree, and to such a degree of comfort to himself, that he found it worthy of celebration. The forms and themes were to his hand, common currency, as we have seen; his own experience provided the insight, the 'judicious knowledge of the worth And dignity of individual man' which makes *Lyrical Ballads* significant literature.

[1] See also the prophecy of the subject-matter he was about to use, *Prel.*, XIII. 221–78.

SELECT BIBLIOGRAPHY
AND
LIST OF ABBREVIATIONS

I. *Original Editions*

L.B.	*Lyrical Ballads, with a few other Poems* (Bristol or London, 1798).
L.B.	*Lyrical Ballads, with other Poems, in two Volumes, by W. Wordsworth* (London, 1800).
L.B.	*Lyrical Ballads, with Pastoral and other Poems, in two Volumes, by W. Wordsworth* (London, 1802, 1805).

II. *Modern Editions*

Hutchinson	Of *L.B.*, 1798: by T. Hutchinson (London, 1898); by H. Littledale (Oxford, 1911); facsimile in Noel Douglas Replicas (London, 1926).
	Of *L.B.*, 1800–5: by G. Sampson (London, 1903); by R. L. Brett and A. R. Jones (London, 1963); by D. Roper (London, 1968).
	Of the Preface to *L.B.*: by W. J. B. Owen (Copenhagen, 1957).
Biog. Lit.	S. T. Coleridge, *Biographia Literaria*, ed. J. Shawcross (Oxford, 1907).
C.L.	*Collected Letters of Samuel Taylor Coleridge*, ed. E. L. Griggs (Oxford, 1956–).
C.N.B.	*Notebooks of Samuel Taylor Coleridge*, ed. K. Coburn (London, 1957–).
C.P.W.	*Poems of Samuel Taylor Coleridge*, ed. E. H. Coleridge (Oxford, 1912).
E.Y.	*Letters of William and Dorothy Wordsworth: The Early Years*, ed. E. de Selincourt. Second edition, revised by Chester L. Shaver (Oxford, 1967).
Journals	*Journals of Dorothy Wordsworth*, ed. E. de Selincourt (London, 1941).
L.Y.	*Letters of William and Dorothy Wordsworth: The Later Years*, ed. E. de Selincourt (Oxford, 1939).

	BIBLIOGRAPHY
M.Y.	*Letters of William and Dorothy Wordsworth: The Middle Years*, ed. E. de Selincourt. Second edition, Part I (1806–11), revised by Mary Moorman (Oxford, 1969), Part II (1812–20), revised by Mary Moorman and Alan G. Hill (Oxford, 1970).
Prel.	*The Prelude*, ed. E. de Selincourt. Second edition, revised by Helen Darbishire (Oxford, 1959).
W.P.W.	*Poetical Works of William Wordsworth*, ed. E. de Selincourt and H. Darbishire (Oxford, 1940–9).

III. *Illustrative and Critical Material*

M. H. Abrams, *The Mirror and the Lamp* (New York, 1953).

— 'Wordsworth and Coleridge on Diction and Figures', *English Institute Essays 1952* (New York, 1954).

Srikumar Banerjee, *Critical Theories and Poetic Practice in the Lyrical Ballads* (London, 1931).

Marjorie L. Barstow, *Wordsworth's Theory of Poetic Diction* (New Haven, 1917).

Arthur Beatty, *William Wordsworth: His Doctrine and Art in their Historical Relations* (Madison, 1922, 1927).

Kathleen Coburn, 'Coleridge and Wordsworth on the Supernatural', *U.T.Q.*, xxv (1956).

Reminiscences	Joseph Cottle, *Reminiscences of . . . Coleridge and . . . Southey* (New York, 1847).
	John F. Danby, *The Simple Wordsworth* (London, 1960).
	Helen Darbishire, *The Poet Wordsworth* (Oxford, 1950).
Foxon	D. F. Foxon, 'The Printing of *Lyrical Ballads*, 1798', *The Library*, 5th series, ix (1954).
	H. W. Garrod, *Wordsworth* (Oxford, 1923, 1927).
Healey	George Harris Healey, *The Cornell Wordsworth Collection* (Ithaca, 1957).
I.F.	Notes on his poems dictated by Wordsworth to Isabella Fenwick in 1843.
	John Jones, *The Egotistical Sublime* (London, 1954).
	Emile Legouis, 'Some Remarks on the Composition of the *Lyrical Ballads* of 1798', in *Wordsworth and*

Coleridge: Studies in Honor of George McLean Harper, ed. E. L. Griggs (Princeton, 1939).

Lowes John Livingston Lowes, *The Road to Xanadu* (London, 1927).

Kenneth MacLean, *Agrarian Age: A Background for Wordsworth* (New Haven, 1950).

H. M. Margoliouth, *Wordsworth and Coleridge 1795–1834* (Oxford, 1953).

Robert Mayo, 'The Contemporaneity of the *Lyrical Ballads*', *P.M.L.A.*, lxix (1954).

Early Years Mary Moorman, *William Wordsworth. A Biography. The Early Years 1770–1803* (Oxford, 1957).

W. J. B. Owen, 'The Major Theme of Wordsworth's 1800 Preface', *E. in C.*, vi (1956).

—*Wordsworth as Critic* (Toronto, 1969).

Stephen M. Parrish, '*The Thorn*: Wordsworth's Dramatic Monologue', *E.L.H.*, xxiv (1957).

— 'The Wordsworth-Coleridge Controversy', *P.M.L.A.*, lxxiii (1958).

— 'Dramatic Technique in the *Lyrical Ballads*', *P.M.L.A.*, lxxiv (1959).

— 'Wordsworth and Coleridge on Meter', *J.E.G.P.*, lix (1960).

Thomas M. Raysor, 'Coleridge's Criticism of Wordsworth', *P.M.L.A.*, liv (1939).

Mark L. Reed, 'Wordsworth, Coleridge, and the "Plan" of the *Lyrical Ballads*', *U.T.Q.*, xxxiv (1965).

Reliques *Reliques of Ancient English Poetry*, ed. T. Percy (London, 1765, &c.).

Charles Ryskamp, 'Wordsworth's *Lyrical Ballads* in their Time', in *From Sensibility to Romanticism: Essays Presented to Frederick A. Pottle*, ed. F. W. Hilles and H. Bloom (New York, 1965).

Roger Sharrock, 'Wordsworth's Revolt against Literature', *E. in C.*, iii (1953).

Roger Sharrock, 'The Chemist and the Poet', *Notes and Records of the Royal Society of London*, xvii (1962).

René Wellek, 'Wordsworth'. In his *History of Modern Criticism 1750–1950*, ii (London, 1955).

George Whalley, 'Preface to *Lyrical Ballads:* A Portent', *U.T.Q.*, xxv (1956).

Carl R. Woodring, *Wordsworth* (Boston, 1965).

LYRICAL BALLADS,

WITH

A FEW OTHER POEMS.

LONDON:
PRINTED FOR J. & A. ARCH, GRACECHURCH-STREET.
1798.

ADVERTISEMENT

It is the honourable characteristic of Poetry that its materials are to be found in every subject which can interest the human mind. The evidence of this fact is to be sought, not in the writings of Critics, but in those of Poets themselves.

The majority of the following poems are to be considered as experiments. They were written chiefly with a view to ascertain how far the language of conversation in the middle and lower classes of society is adapted to the purposes of poetic pleasure. Readers accustomed to the gaudiness and inane phraseology of many modern writers, if they persist in reading this book to its conclusion, will perhaps frequently have to struggle with feelings of strangeness and aukwardness: they will look round for poetry, and will be induced to enquire by what species of courtesy these attempts can be permitted to assume that title. It is desirable that such readers, for their own sakes, should not suffer the solitary word Poetry, a word of very disputed meaning, to stand in the way of their gratification; but that, while they are perusing this book, they should ask themselves if it contains a natural delineation of human passions, human characters, and human incidents; and if the answer be favorable to the author's wishes, that they should consent to be pleased in spite of that most dreadful enemy to our pleasures, our own pre-established codes of decision.

Readers of superior judgment may disapprove of the style in which many of these pieces are executed it must be expected that many lines and phrases will not exactly suit their taste. It will perhaps appear to them, that wishing to avoid the prevalent fault of the day, the author has sometimes descended too low, and that many of his expressions are too familiar, and not of sufficient dignity. It is apprehended, that the more conversant the reader is with our elder writers, and with those in modern times who have been the most successful in painting manners and passions, the fewer complaints of this kind will he have to make.

An accurate taste in poetry, and in all the other arts, Sir Joshua Reynolds has observed, is an acquired talent, which can only be produced by severe thought, and a long continued intercourse with the best models of composition. This is mentioned not with so ridiculous a purpose as to prevent the most inexperienced reader from judging for himself; but merely to temper the rashness of decision, and to suggest that if poetry be a subject on which much time has not been bestowed, the judgment may be erroneous, and that in many cases it necessarily will be so.

The tale of Goody Blake and Harry Gill is founded on a well-authenticated fact which happened in Warwickshire. Of the other poems in the collection, it may be proper to say that they are either absolute inventions of the author, or facts which took place within his personal observation or that of his friends. The poem of the Thorn, as the reader will soon discover, is not supposed to be spoken in the author's own person: the character of the loquacious narrator will sufficiently shew itself in the course of the story. The Rime of the Ancyent Marinere was professedly written in imitation of the *style*, as well as of the spirit of the elder poets; but with a few exceptions, the Author believes that the language adopted in it has been equally intelligible for these three last centuries. The lines entitled Expostulation and Reply, and those which follow, arose out of conversation with a friend who was somewhat unreasonably attached to modern books of moral philosophy.

CONTENTS

The Rime of the Ancyent Marinere	7
The Foster-Mother's Tale	32
Lines left upon a Seat in a Yew-tree which stands near the Lake of Esthwaite	35
The Nightingale, a Conversational Poem	37
The Female Vagrant	41
Goody Blake and Harry Gill	50
Lines written at a small distance from my House, and sent by my little Boy to the Person to whom they are addressed	55
Simon Lee, the old Huntsman	57
Anecdote for Fathers	60
We are seven	63
Lines written in early spring	65
The Thorn	66
The last of the Flock	76
The Dungeon	80
The Mad Mother	81
The Idiot Boy	84
Lines written near Richmond, upon the Thames, at Evening	101
Expostulation and Reply	103
The Tables turned; an Evening Scene, on the same subject	104
Old Man travelling	105
The Complaint of a forsaken Indian Woman	106
The Convict	109
Lines written a few miles above Tintern Abbey	111

The Rime of the Ancyent Marinere

IN SEVEN PARTS

ARGUMENT

How a Ship having passed the Line was driven by Storms to the cold Country towards the South Pole; and how from thence she made her course to the tropical Latitude of the Great Pacific Ocean; and of the strange things that befell; and in what manner the Ancyent Marinere came back to his own Country.

I

It is an ancyent Marinere,
   And he stoppeth one of three:
'By thy long grey beard and thy glittering eye
   'Now wherefore stoppest me?

'The Bridegroom's doors are open'd wide
   'And I am next of kin;
'The Guests are met, the Feast is set,—
   'May'st hear the merry din.

But still he holds the wedding-guest—
   There was a Ship, quoth he—
'Nay, if thou'st got a laughsome tale,
   'Marinere! come with me.'

He holds him with his skinny hand,
   Quoth he, there was a Ship—

8   THE RIME OF THE ANCYENT MARINERE

'Now get thee hence, thou grey-beard Loon!
'Or my Staff shall make thee skip.

He holds him with his glittering eye—
   The wedding guest stood still
And listens like a three year's child;
   The Marinere hath his will.   20

The wedding-guest sate on a stone,
   He cannot chuse but hear:
And thus spake on that ancyent man,
   The bright-eyed Marinere.

The Ship was cheer'd, the Harbour clear'd—
   Merrily did we drop
Below the Kirk, below the Hill,
   Below the Light-house top.

The Sun came up upon the left,
   Out of the Sea came he: 30
And he shone bright, and on the right
   Went down into the Sea.

Higher and higher every day,
   Till over the mast at noon—
The wedding-guest here beat his breast,
   For he heard the loud bassoon.

The Bride hath pac'd into the Hall,
   Red as a rose is she;
Nodding their heads before her goes
   The merry Minstralsy.   40

The wedding-guest he beat his breast,
  Yet he cannot chuse but hear:
And thus spake on that ancyent Man,
  The bright-eyed Marinere.

Listen, Stranger! Storm and Wind,
  A Wind and Tempest strong!
For days and weeks it play'd us freaks—
  Like Chaff we drove along.

Listen, Stranger! Mist and Snow,
  And it grew wond'rous cauld:
And Ice mast-high came floating by
  As green as Emerauld.

And thro' the drifts the snowy clifts
  Did send a dismal sheen;
Ne shapes of men ne beasts we ken—
  The Ice was all between.

The Ice was here, the Ice was there,
  The Ice was all around:
It crack'd and growl'd, and roar'd and howl'd—
  Like noises of a swound.

At length did cross an Albatross,
  Thorough the Fog it came;
And an it were a Christian Soul,
  We hail'd it in God's name.

The Marineres gave it biscuit-worms,
  And round and round it flew:
The Ice did split with a Thunder-fit;
  The Helmsman steer'd us thro'.

And a good south wind sprung up behind,
  The Albatross did follow;
And every day for food or play
  Came to the Marinere's hollo!

In mist or cloud on mast or shroud
  It perch'd for vespers nine,
Whiles all the night thro' fog-smoke white
  Glimmer'd the white moon-shine.

'God save thee, ancyent Marinere!
  'From the fiends that plague thee thus—
'Why look'st thou so?'—with my cross bow
  I shot the Albatross.

II

The Sun came up upon the right,
  Out of the Sea came he;
And broad as a weft upon the left
  Went down into the Sea.

And the good south wind still blew behind,
  But no sweet Bird did follow
Ne any day for food or play
  Came to the Marinere's hollo!

And I had done an hellish thing
  And it would work 'em woe:
For all averr'd, I had kill'd the Bird
  That made the Breeze to blow.

Ne dim ne red, like God's own head,
  The glorious Sun uprist:

Then all averr'd, I had kill'd the Bird
  That brought the fog and mist.
'Twas right, said they, such birds to slay
  That bring the fog and mist.

The breezes blew, the white foam flew,
  The furrow follow'd free: 100
We were the first that ever burst
  Into that silent Sea.

Down dropt the breeze, the Sails dropt down,
  'Twas sad as sad could be
And we did speak only to break
  The silence of the Sea.

All in a hot and copper sky
  The bloody sun at noon,
Right up above the mast did stand,
  No bigger than the moon.   110

Day after day, day after day,
  We stuck, ne breath ne motion,
As idle as a painted Ship
  Upon a painted Ocean.

Water, water, every where
  And all the boards did shrink;
Water, water, every where
  Ne any drop to drink.

The very deeps did rot: O Christ!
  That ever this should be!   120
Yea, slimy things did crawl with legs
  Upon the slimy Sea.

About, about, in reel and rout
   The Death-fires danc'd at night;
The water, like a witch's oils,
   Burnt green and blue and white.

And some in dreams assured were
   Of the Spirit that plagued us so:
Nine fathom deep he had follow'd us
   From the Land of Mist and Snow.   130

And every tongue thro' utter drouth
   Was wither'd at the root;
We could not speak no more than if
   We had been choked with soot.

Ah wel-a-day! what evil looks
   Had I from old and young;
Instead of the Cross the Albatross
   About my neck was hung.

III

I saw a something in the Sky
   No bigger than my fist;   140
At first it seem'd a little speck
   And then it seem'd a mist:
It mov'd and mov'd, and took at last
   A certain shape, I wist.

A speck, a mist, a shape, I wist!
   And still it ner'd and ner'd;
And, an it dodg'd a water-sprite,
   It plung'd and tack'd and veer'd.

With throat unslack'd, with black lips bak'd
    Ne could we laugh, ne wail: 150
Then while thro' drouth all dumb they stood
I bit my arm and suck'd the blood
    And cry'd, A sail! a sail!

With throat unslack'd, with black lips bak'd
    Agape they hear'd me call:
Gramercy! they for joy did grin
And all at once their breath drew in
    As they were drinking all.

She doth not tack from side to side—
    Hither to work us weal   160
Withouten wind, withouten tide
    She steddies with upright keel.

The western wave was all a flame,
    The day was well nigh done!
Almost upon the western wave
    Rested the broad bright Sun;
When that strange shape drove suddenly
    Betwixt us and the Sun.

And strait the Sun was fleck'd with bars
    (Heaven's mother send us grace)   170
As if thro' a dungeon grate he peer'd
    With broad and burning face.

Alas! (thought I, and my heart beat loud)
    How fast she neres and neres!
Are those *her* Sails that glance in the Sun
    Like restless gossameres?

Are these *her* naked ribs, which fleck'd
   The sun that did behind them peer?
And are these two all, all the crew,
   That woman and her fleshless Pheere? 180

His bones were black with many a crack,
   All black and bare, I ween;
Jet-black and bare, save where with rust
Of mouldy damps and charnel crust
   They're patch'd with purple and green.

Her lips are red, *her* looks are free,
   Her locks are yellow as gold:
Her skin is as white as leprosy,
And she is far liker Death than he;
   Her flesh makes the still air cold. 190

The naked Hulk alongside came
   And the Twain were playing dice;
'The Game is done! I've won, I've won!'
   Quoth she, and whistled thrice.

A gust of wind sterte up behind
   And whistled thro' his bones;
Thro' the holes of his eyes and the hole of his mouth
   Half-whistles and half-groans.

With never a whisper in the Sea
   Off darts the Spectre-ship; 200
While clombe above the Eastern bar
The horned Moon, with one bright Star
   Almost atween the tips.

One after one by the horned Moon
 (Listen, O Stranger! to me)
Each turn'd his face with a ghastly pang
 And curs'd me with his ee.

Four times fifty living men,
 With never a sigh or groan,
With heavy thump, a lifeless lump
 They dropp'd down one by one.

Their souls did from their bodies fly,—
 They fled to bliss or woe;
And every soul it pass'd me by,
 Like the whiz of my Cross-bow.

IV

'I fear thee, ancyent Marinere!
 'I fear thy skinny hand;
'And thou art long and lank and brown
 'As is the ribb'd Sea-sand.

'I fear thee and thy glittering eye
 'And thy skinny hand so brown—
Fear not, fear not, thou wedding guest!
 This body dropt not down.

Alone, alone, all all alone
 Alone on the wide wide Sea;
And Christ would take no pity on
 My soul in agony.

The many men so beautiful,
 And they all dead did lie!

And a million million slimy things 230
  Liv'd on—and so did I.

I look'd upon the rotting Sea,
  And drew my eyes away;
I look'd upon the eldritch deck,
  And there the dead men lay.

I look'd to Heaven, and try'd to pray;
  But or ever a prayer had gusht,
A wicked whisper came and made
  My heart as dry as dust.

I clos'd my lids and kept them close, 240
  Till the balls like pulses beat;
For the sky and the sea, and the sea and the sky
Lay like a load on my weary eye,
  And the dead were at my feet.

The cold sweat melted from their limbs,
  Ne rot, ne reek did they;
The look with which they look'd on me,
  Had never pass'd away.

An orphan's curse would drag to Hell
  A spirit from on high: 250
But O! more horrible than that
  Is the curse in a dead man's eye!
Seven days, seven nights I saw that curse,
  And yet I could not die.

The moving Moon went up the sky
  And no where did abide:

THE RIME OF THE ANCYENT MARINERE

Softly she was going up
   And a star or two beside

Her beams bemock'd the sultry main
   Like morning frosts yspread; 260
But where the ship's huge shadow lay,
The charmed water burnt alway
   A still and awful red.

Beyond the shadow of the ship
   I watch'd the water-snakes:
They mov'd in tracks of shining white;
And when they rear'd, the elfish light
   Fell off in hoary flakes.

Within the shadow of the ship
   I watch'd their rich attire: 270
Blue, glossy green, and velvet black
They coil'd and swam; and every track
   Was a flash of golden fire.

O happy living things! no tongue
   Their beauty might declare:
A spring of love gusht from my heart,
   And I bless'd them unaware!
Sure my kind saint took pity on me,
   And I bless'd them unaware.

The self-same moment I could pray; 280
   And from my neck so free
The Albatross fell off, and sank
   Like lead into the sea.

V

O sleep, it is a gentle thing
  Belov'd from pole to pole!
To Mary-queen the praise be yeven
She sent the gentle sleep from heaven
  That slid into my soul.

The silly buckets on the deck
  That had so long remain'd,
I dreamt that they were fill'd with dew
  And when I awoke it rain'd.

My lips were wet, my throat was cold,
  My garments all were dank;
Sure I had drunken in my dreams
  And still my body drank.

I mov'd and could not feel my limbs,
  I was so light, almost
I thought that I had died in sleep,
  And was a blessed Ghost.

The roaring wind! it roar'd far off,
  It did not come anear;
But with its sound it shook the sails
  That were so thin and sere.

The upper air bursts into life,
  And a hundred fire-flags sheen
To and fro they are hurried about;
And to and fro, and in and out
  The stars dance on between.

THE RIME OF THE ANCYENT MARINERE

The coming wind doth roar more loud; 310
   The sails do sigh, like sedge:
The rain pours down from one black cloud
   And the Moon is at its edge.

Hark! hark! the thick black cloud is cleft,
   And the Moon is at its side:
Like waters shot from some high crag,
The lightning falls with never a jag
   A river steep and wide.

The strong wind reach'd the ship: it roar'd
   And dropp'd down, like a stone! 320
Beneath the lightning and the moon
   The dead men gave a groan.

They groan'd, they stirr'd, they all uprose,
   Ne spake, ne mov'd their eyes:
It had been strange, even in a dream
   To have seen those dead men rise.

The helmsman steerd, the ship mov'd on;
   Yet never a breeze up-blew;
The Marineres all 'gan work the ropes,
   Where they were wont to do: 330
They rais'd their limbs like lifeless tools—
   We were a ghastly crew.

The body of my brother's son
   Stood by me knee to knee:
The body and I pull'd at one rope,
   But he said nought to me—
And I quak'd to think of my own voice
   How frightful it would be!

The day-light dawn'd—they dropp'd their arms,
   And cluster'd round the mast: 340
Sweet sounds rose slowly thro' their mouths
   And from their bodies pass'd.

Around, around, flew each sweet sound,
   Then darted to the sun:
Slowly the sounds came back again
   Now mix'd, now one by one.

Sometimes a dropping from the sky
   I heard the Lavrock sing;
Sometimes all little birds that are
How they seem'd to fill the sea and air   350
   With their sweet jargoning,

And now 'twas like all instruments,
   Now like a lonely flute;
And now it is an angel's song
   That makes the heavens be mute.

It ceas'd: yet still the sails made on
   A pleasant noise till noon,
A noise like of a hidden brook
   In the leafy month of June,
That to the sleeping woods all night   360
   Singeth a quiet tune.

Listen, O listen, thou Wedding-guest!
   'Marinere! thou hast thy will:
'For that, which comes out of thine eye, doth make
   'My body and soul to be still.'

Never sadder tale was told
  To a man of woman born:
Sadder and wiser thou wedding-guest!
  Thou'lt rise to morrow morn.

Never sadder tale was heard
  By a man of woman born:
The Marineres all return'd to work
  As silent as beforne.

The Marineres all 'gan pull the ropes,
  But look at me they n'old:
Thought I, I am as thin as air—
  They cannot me behold.

Till noon we silently sail'd on
  Yet never a breeze did breathe:
Slowly and smoothly went the ship
  Mov'd onward from beneath.

Under the keel nine fathom deep
  From the land of mist and snow
The spirit slid: and it was He
  That made the Ship to go.
The sails at noon left off their tune
  And the Ship stood still also.

The sun right up above the mast
  Had fix'd her to the ocean:
But in a minute she 'gan stir
  With a short uneasy motion—
Backwards and forwards half her length
  With a short uneasy motion.

Then, like a pawing horse let go,
  She made a sudden bound:
It flung the blood into my head,
  And I fell into a swound.

How long in that same fit I lay,
  I have not to declare;
But ere my living life return'd,
I heard and in my soul discern'd
  Two voices in the air,

'Is it he?' quoth one, 'Is this the man?
  'By him who died on cross,
'With his cruel bow he lay'd full low
  'The harmless Albatross.

'The spirit who 'bideth by himself
  'In the land of mist and snow,
'He lov'd the bird that lov'd the man
  'Who shot him with his bow.

The other was a softer voice,
  As soft as honey-dew:
Quoth he the man hath penance done,
  And penance more will do.

VI

First Voice
'But tell me, tell me! speak again,
  'Thy soft response renewing—
'What makes that ship drive on so fast?
  'What is the Ocean doing?

SECOND VOICE
'Still as a Slave before his Lord,
  'The Ocean hath no blast:
'His great bright eye most silently
  'Up to the moon is cast—

'If he may know which way to go,
  'For she guides him smooth or grim.
'See, brother, see! how graciously
  'She looketh down on him.

FIRST VOICE
'But why drives on that ship so fast
  'Withouten wave or wind?

SECOND VOICE
'The air is cut away before,
  'And closes from behind.

'Fly, brother, fly! more high, more high,
  'Or we shall be belated:
'For slow and slow that ship will go,
  'When the Marinere's trance is abated.'

I woke, and we were sailing on
  As in a gentle weather:
'Twas night, calm night, the moon was high;
  The dead men stood together.

All stood together on the deck,
  For a charnel-dungeon fitter:
All fix'd on me their stony eyes
  That in the moon did glitter.

The pang, the curse, with which they died,
   Had never pass'd away:
I could not draw my een from theirs
   Ne turn them up to pray.

And in its time the spell was snapt,
   And I could move my een:
I look'd far-forth, but little saw
   Of what might else be seen.   450

Like one, that on a lonely road
   Doth walk in fear and dread,
And having once turn'd round, walks on
   And turns no more his head:
Because he knows, a frightful fiend
   Doth close behind him tread.

But soon there breath'd a wind on me,
   Ne sound ne motion made:
Its path was not upon the sea
   In ripple or in shade.   460

It rais'd my hair, it fann'd my cheek,
   Like a meadow-gale of spring—
It mingled strangely with my fears,
   Yet it felt like a welcoming.

Swiftly, swiftly flew the ship,
   Yet she sail'd softly too:
Sweetly, sweetly blew the breeze—
   On me alone it blew.

O dream of joy! is this indeed
   The light-house top I see?   470

Is this the Hill? Is this the Kirk?
  Is this mine own countrée?

We drifted o'er the Harbour-bar,
  And I with sobs did pray—
'O let me be awake, my God!
  'Or let me sleep alway!'

The harbour-bay was clear as glass,
  So smoothly it was strewn!
And on the bay the moon light lay,
  And the shadow of the moon.   480

The moonlight bay was white all o'er,
  Till rising from the same,
Full many shapes, that shadows were,
  Like as of torches came.

A little distance from the prow
  Those dark-red shadows were;
But soon I saw that my own flesh
  Was red as in a glare.

I turn'd my head in fear and dread,
  And by the holy rood,   490
The bodies had advanc'd, and now
  Before the mast they stood.

They lifted up their stiff right arms,
  They held them strait and tight;
And each right-arm burnt like a torch,
  A torch that's borne upright.
Their stony eye-balls glitter'd on
  In the red and smoky light.

I pray'd and turn'd my head away
  Forth looking as before. 500
There was no breeze upon the bay,
  No wave against the shore.

The rock shone bright, the kirk no less
  That stands above the rock:
The moonlight steep'd in silentness
  The steady weathercock.

And the bay was white with silent light,
  Till rising from the same
Full many shapes, that shadows were,
  In crimson colours came. 510

A little distance from the prow
  Those crimson shadows were:
I turn'd my eyes upon the deck—
  O Christ! what saw I there?

Each corse lay flat, lifeless and flat;
  And by the Holy rood
A man all light, a seraph-man,
  On every corse there stood.

This seraph-band, each wav'd his hand:
  It was a heavenly sight: 520
They stood as signals to the land,
  Each one a lovely light:

This seraph-band, each wav'd his hand,
  No voice did they impart—

No voice; but O! the silence sank,
  Like music on my heart.

Eftsones I heard the dash of oars,
  I heard the pilot's cheer:
My head was turn'd perforce away
  And I saw a boat appear. 530

Then vanish'd all the lovely lights;
  The bodies rose anew:
With silent pace, each to his place,
  Came back the ghastly crew.
The wind, that shade nor motion made,
  On me alone it blew.

The pilot, and the pilot's boy
  I heard them coming fast:
Dear Lord in Heaven! it was a joy,
  The dead men could not blast. 540

I saw a third—I heard his voice:
  It is the Hermit good!
He singeth loud his godly hymns
  That he makes in the wood.
He'll shrieve my soul, he'll wash away
  The Albatross's blood.

VII

This Hermit good lives in that wood
  Which slopes down to the Sea.
How loudly his sweet voice he rears!

He loves to talk with Marineres 550
   That come from a far Contrée.

He kneels at morn and noon and eve—
   He hath a cushion plump:
It is the moss, that wholly hides
   The rotted old Oak-stump.

The Skiff-boat ne'rd: I heard them talk,
   'Why, this is strange, I trow!
'Where are those lights so many and fair
   'That signal made but now?

'Strange, by my faith! the Hermit said— 560
   'And they answer'd not our cheer.
'The planks look warp'd, and see those sails
   'How thin they are and sere!
'I never saw aught like to them
   'Unless perchance it were

'The skeletons of leaves that lag
   'My forest brook along:
'When the Ivy-tod is heavy with snow,
'And the Owlet whoops to the wolf below
   'That eats the she-wolf's young. 570

'Dear Lord! it has a fiendish look—
   (The Pilot made reply)
'I am a-fear'd.—'Push on, push on!
   'Said the Hermit cheerily.

The Boat came closer to the Ship,
    But I ne spake ne stirr'd!
The Boat came close beneath the Ship,
    And strait a sound was heard!

Under the water it rumbled on,
    Still louder and more dread: 580
It reach'd the Ship, it split the bay;
    The Ship went down like lead.

Stunn'd by that loud and dreadful sound,
    Which sky and ocean smote:
Like one that hath been seven days drown'd
    My body lay afloat:
But, swift as dreams, myself I found
    Within the Pilot's boat.

Upon the whirl, where sank the Ship,
    The boat spun round and round: 590
And all was still, save that the hill
    Was telling of the sound.

I mov'd my lips: the Pilot shriek'd
    And fell down in a fit.
The Holy Hermit rais'd his eyes
    And pray'd where he did sit.

I took the oars: the Pilot's boy,
    Who now doth crazy go,
Laugh'd loud and long, and all the while
    His eyes went to and fro,   600

'Ha! ha!' quoth he—'full plain I see,
'The devil knows how to row.'

And now all in mine own Countrée
 I stood on the firm land!
The Hermit stepp'd forth from the boat,
 And scarcely he could stand.

'O shrieve me, shrieve me, holy Man!
 The Hermit cross'd his brow—
'Say quick,' quoth he, 'I bid thee say
 'What manner man art thou? 610

Forthwith this frame of mine was wrench'd
 With a woeful agony,
Which forc'd me to begin my tale
 And then it left me free.

Since then at an uncertain hour,
 Now oftimes and now fewer,
That anguish comes and makes me tell
 My ghastly aventure.

I pass, like night, from land to land;
 I have strange power of speech; 620
The moment that his face I see
I know the man that must hear me;
 To him my tale I teach.

What loud uproar bursts from that door!
 The Wedding-guests are there;

But in the Garden-bower the Bride
  And Bride-maids singing are:
And hark the little Vesper-bell
  Which biddeth me to prayer.

O Wedding-guest! this soul hath been
  Alone on a wide wide sea:
So lonely 'twas, that God himself
  Scarce seemed there to be.

O sweeter than the Marriage-feast,
  'Tis sweeter far to me
To walk together to the Kirk
  With a goodly company.

To walk together to the Kirk
  And all together pray,
While each to his great father bends,
Old men, and babes, and loving friends,
  And Youths, and Maidens gay.

Farewell, farewell! but this I tell
  To thee, thou wedding-guest!
He prayeth well who loveth well
  Both man and bird and beast.

He prayeth best who loveth best,
  All things both great and small:
For the dear God, who loveth us,
  He made and loveth all.

THE RIME OF THE ANCYENT MARINERE

> The Marinere, whose eye is bright,
> 	Whose beard with age is hoar,
> Is gone; and now the wedding-guest
> 	Turn'd from the bridegroom's door.
>
> He went, like one that hath been stunn'd
> 	And is of sense forlorn:
> A sadder and a wiser man
> 	He rose the morrow morn.

The Foster-Mother's Tale

A DRAMATIC FRAGMENT

FOSTER-MOTHER

I never saw the man whom you describe.

MARIA

'Tis strange! he spake of you familiarly
As mine and Albert's common Foster-mother.

FOSTER-MOTHER

Now blessings on the man, whoe'er he be,
That joined your names with mine! O my sweet lady,
As often as I think of those dear times
When you two little ones would stand at eve
On each side of my chair, and make me learn
All you had learnt in the day; and how to talk
In gentle phrase, then bid me sing to you—   10
'Tis more like heaven to come than what *has* been.

MARIA

O my dear Mother! this strange man has left me
Troubled with wilder fancies, than the moon
Breeds in the love-sick maid who gazes at it,
Till lost in inward vision, with wet eye
She gazes idly!—But that entrance, Mother!

FOSTER-MOTHER

Can no one hear? It is a perilous tale!

MARIA

No one.

FOSTER-MOTHER

    My husband's father told it me,
Poor old Leoni!—Angels rest his soul!
He was a woodman, and could fell and saw
With lusty arm. You know that huge round beam
Which props the hanging wall of the old chapel?
Beneath that tree, while yet it was a tree
He found a baby wrapt in mosses, lined
With thistle-beards, and such small locks of wool
As hang on brambles. Well, he brought him home,
And reared him at the then Lord Velez' cost.
And so the babe grew up a pretty boy,
A pretty boy, but most unteachable—
And never learnt a prayer, nor told a bead,
But knew the names of birds, and mocked their notes,
And whistled, as he were a bird himself:
And all the autumn 'twas his only play
To get the seeds of wild flowers, and to plant them
With earth and water, on the stumps of trees.

THE FOSTER-MOTHER'S TALE

A Friar, who gathered simples in the wood,
A grey-haired man—he loved this little boy,
The boy loved him—and, when the Friar taught him,
He soon could write with the pen: and from that time,
Lived chiefly at the Convent or the Castle. 40
So he became a very learned youth.
But Oh! poor wretch!—he read, and read, and read,
'Till his brain turned—and ere his twentieth year,
He had unlawful thoughts of many things:
And though he prayed, he never loved to pray
With holy men, nor in a holy place—
But yet his speech, it was so soft and sweet,
The late Lord Velez ne'er was wearied with him.
And once, as by the north side of the Chapel
They stood together, chained in deep discourse, 50
The earth heaved under them with such a groan,
That the wall tottered, and had well-nigh fallen
Right on their heads. My Lord was sorely frightened;
A fever seized him, and he made confession
Of all the heretical and lawless talk
Which brought this judgment: so the youth was seized
And cast into that hole. My husband's father
Sobbed like a child—it almost broke his heart:
And once as he was working in the cellar,
He heard a voice distinctly; 'twas the youth's, 60
Who sung a doleful song about green fields,
How sweet it were on lake or wild savannah,
To hunt for food, and be a naked man,
And wander up and down at liberty.
He always doted on the youth, and now
His love grew desperate; and defying death,
He made that cunning entrance I described:
And the young man escaped.

MARIA
'Tis a sweet tale:
Such as would lull a listening child to sleep,
His rosy face besoiled with unwiped tears.— 70
And what became of him?

FOSTER-MOTHER
                            He went on ship-board
With those bold voyagers, who made discovery
Of golden lands. Leoni's younger brother
Went likewise, and when he returned to Spain,
He told Leoni, that the poor mad youth,
Soon after they arrived in that new world,
In spite of his dissuasion, seized a boat,
And all alone, set sail by silent moonlight
Up a great river, great as any sea,
And ne'er was heard of more: but 'tis supposed, 80
He lived and died among the savage men.

Lines left upon a Seat in a Yew-tree

WHICH STANDS NEAR THE LAKE OF ESTHWAITE,
ON A DESOLATE PART OF THE SHORE,
YET COMMANDING A BEAUTIFUL PROSPECT

—Nay, Traveller! rest. This lonely yew-tree stands
Far from all human dwelling: what if here
No sparkling rivulet spread the verdant herb;
What if these barren boughs the bee not loves;
Yet, if the wind breathe soft, the curling waves,
That break against the shore, shall lull thy mind
By one soft impulse saved from vacancy.

———————————Who he was
That piled these stones, and with the mossy sod
First covered o'er, and taught this aged tree,
Now wild, to bend its arms in circling shade,
I well remember.—He was one who own'd
No common soul. In youth, by genius nurs'd,
And big with lofty views, he to the world
Went forth, pure in his heart, against the taint
Of dissolute tongues, 'gainst jealousy, and hate,
And scorn, against all enemies prepared,
All but neglect: and so, his spirit damped
At once, with rash disdain he turned away,
And with the food of pride sustained his soul
In solitude.—Stranger! these gloomy boughs
Had charms for him; and here he loved to sit,
His only visitants a straggling sheep,
The stone-chat, or the glancing sand-piper;
And on these barren rocks, with juniper,
And heath, and thistle, thinly sprinkled o'er,
Fixing his downward eye, he many an hour
A morbid pleasure nourished, tracing here
An emblem of his own unfruitful life:
And lifting up his head, he then would gaze
On the more distant scene; how lovely 'tis
Thou seest, and he would gaze till it became
Far lovelier, and his heart could not sustain
The beauty still more beauteous. Nor, that time,
Would he forget those beings, to whose minds,
Warm from the labours of benevolence,
The world, and man himself, appeared a scene
Of kindred loveliness: then he would sigh
With mournful joy, to think that others felt
What he must never feel: and so, lost man!

LINES LEFT UPON A SEAT

On visionary views would fancy feed,
Till his eye streamed with tears. In this deep vale
He died, this seat his only monument.

If thou be one whose heart the holy forms
Of young imagination have kept pure,
Stranger! henceforth be warned; and know, that pride,
Howe'er disguised in its own majesty,
Is littleness; that he, who feels contempt
For any living thing, hath faculties
Which he has never used; that thought with him   50
Is in its infancy. The man, whose eye
Is ever on himself, doth look on one,
The least of nature's works, one who might move
The wise man to that scorn which wisdom holds
Unlawful, ever. O, be wiser thou!
Instructed that true knowledge leads to love,
True dignity abides with him alone
Who, in the silent hour of inward thought,
Can still suspect, and still revere himself,
In lowliness of heart.   60

The Nightingale

A CONVERSATIONAL POEM, WRITTEN IN APRIL, 1798

No cloud, no relique of the sunken day
Distinguishes the West, no long thin slip
Of sullen Light, no obscure trembling hues.
Come, we will rest on this old mossy Bridge!
You see the glimmer of the stream beneath.

But hear no murmuring: it flows silently
O'er its soft bed of verdure. All is still,
A balmy night! and tho' the stars be dim,
Yet let us think upon the vernal showers
That gladden the green earth, and we shall find   10
A pleasure in the dimness of the stars.
And hark! the Nightingale begins its song,
'Most musical, most melancholy'* Bird!
A melancholy Bird? O idle thought!
In nature there is nothing melancholy.
—But some night-wandering Man, whose heart was pierc'd
With the remembrance of a grievous wrong,
Or slow distemper or neglected love,
(And so, poor Wretch! fill'd all things with himself
And made all gentle sounds tell back the tale   20
Of his own sorrows) he and such as he
First nam'd these notes a melancholy strain;
And many a poet echoes the conceit,
Poet, who hath been building up the rhyme
When he had better far have stretch'd his limbs
Beside a brook in mossy forest-dell
By sun or moonlight, to the influxes
Of shapes and sounds and shifting elements
Surrendering his whole spirit, of his song
And of his fame forgetful! so his fame   30
Should share in nature's immortality,
A venerable thing! and so his song

* '*Most musical, most melancholy.*' This passage in Milton possesses an excellence far superior to that of mere description: it is spoken in the character of the melancholy Man, and has therefore a *dramatic* propriety. The Author makes this remark, to rescue himself from the charge of having alluded with levity to a line in Milton: a charge than which none could be more painful to him, except perhaps that of having ridiculed his Bible.

Should make all nature lovelier, and itself
Be lov'd, like nature!—But 'twill not be so;
And youths and maidens most poetical
Who lose the deep'ning twilights of the spring
In ball-rooms and hot theatres, they still
Full of meek sympathy must heave their sighs
O'er Philomela's pity-pleading strains.
My Friend, and my Friend's Sister! we have learnt
A different lore: we may not thus profane
Nature's sweet voices always full of love
And joyance! 'Tis the merry Nightingale
That crowds, and hurries, and precipitates
With fast thick warble his delicious notes,
As he were fearful, that an April night
Would be too short for him to utter forth
His love-chant, and disburthen his full soul
Of all its music! And I know a grove
Of large extent, hard by a castle huge
Which the great lord inhabits not: and so
This grove is wild with tangling underwood,
And the trim walks are broken up, and grass,
Thin grass and king-cups grow within the paths.
But never elsewhere in one place I knew
So many Nightingales: and far and near
In wood and thicket over the wide grove
They answer and provoke each other's songs—
With skirmish and capricious passagings,
And murmurs musical and swift jug jug
And one low piping sound more sweet than all—
Stirring the air with such an harmony,
That should you close your eyes, you might almost
Forget it was not day! On moonlight bushes,
Whose dewy leafits are but half disclos'd,

You may perchance behold them on the twigs,
Their bright, bright eyes, their eyes both bright and full,
Glistning, while many a glow-worm in the shade
Lights up her love-torch.

                    A most gentle maid
Who dwelleth in her hospitable home
Hard by the Castle, and at latest eve,
(Even like a Lady vow'd and dedicate
To something more than nature in the grove)
Glides thro' the pathways; she knows all their notes,
That gentle Maid! and oft, a moment's space,
What time the moon was lost behind a cloud,
Hath heard a pause of silence: till the Moon
Emerging, hath awaken'd earth and sky
With one sensation, and those wakeful Birds
Have all burst forth in choral minstrelsy,
As if one quick and sudden Gale had swept
An hundred airy harps! And she hath watch'd
Many a Nightingale perch giddily
On blosmy twig still swinging from the breeze,
And to that motion tune his wanton song,
Like tipsy Joy that reels with tossing head.

Farewell, O Warbler! till to-morrow eve,
And you, my friends! farewell, a short farewell!
We have been loitering long and pleasantly,
And now for our dear homes.—That strain again!
Full fain it would delay me!—My dear Babe,
Who, capable of no articulate sound,
Mars all things with his imitative lisp,
How he would place his hand beside his ear,
His little hand, the small forefinger up,

And bid us listen! And I deem it wise
To make him Nature's playmate. He knows well
The evening star: and once when he awoke
In most distressful mood (some inward pain
Had made up that strange thing, an infant's dream) 100
I hurried with him to our orchard plot,
And he beholds the moon, and hush'd at once
Suspends his sobs, and laughs most silently,
While his fair eyes that swam with undropt tears
Did glitter in the yellow moon-beam! Well—
It is a father's tale. But if that Heaven
Should give me life, his childhood shall grow up
Familiar with these songs, that with the night
He may associate Joy! Once more farewell,
Sweet Nightingale! once more, my friends! farewell. 110

The Female Vagrant

By Derwent's side my Father's cottage stood,
(The Woman thus her artless story told)
One field, a flock, and what the neighbouring flood
Supplied, to him were more than mines of gold.
Light was my sleep; my days in transport roll'd:
With thoughtless joy I stretch'd along the shore
My father's nets, or watched, when from the fold
High o'er the cliffs I led my fleecy store,
A dizzy depth below! his boat and twinkling oar.

My father was a good and pious man, 10
An honest man by honest parents bred,
And I believe that, soon as I began
To lisp, he made me kneel beside my bed,

And in his hearing there my prayers I said:
And afterwards, by my good father taught,
I read, and loved the books in which I read;
For books in every neighbouring house I sought,
And nothing to my mind a sweeter pleasure brought.

Can I forget what charms did once adorn
My garden, stored with pease, and mint, and thyme,   20
And rose and lilly for the sabbath morn?
The sabbath bells, and their delightful chime;
The gambols and wild freaks at shearing time;
My hens's rich nest through long grass scarce espied;
The cowslip-gathering at May's dewy prime;
The swans, that, when I sought the water-side,
From far to meet me came, spreading their snowy pride.

The staff I yet remember which upbore
The bending body of my active sire;
His seat beneath the honeyed sycamore   30
When the bees hummed, and chair by winter fire;
When market-morning came, the neat attire
With which, though bent on haste, myself I deck'd;
My watchful dog, whose starts of furious ire,
When stranger passed, so often I have check'd;
The red-breast known for years, which at my casement
   peck'd.

The suns of twenty summers danced along,—
Ah! little marked, how fast they rolled away:
Then rose a mansion proud our woods among,
And cottage after cottage owned its sway,   40
No joy to see a neighbouring house, or stray
Through pastures not his own, the master took;

THE FEMALE VAGRANT

My Father dared his greedy wish gainsay;
He loved his old hereditary nook,
And ill could I the thought of such sad parting brook.

But, when he had refused the proffered gold,
To cruel injuries he became a prey,
Sore-traversed in whate'er he bought and sold:
His troubles grew upon him day by day,
Till all his substance fell into decay.   50
His little range of water was denied;*
All but the bed where his old body lay,
All, all was seized, and weeping, side by side,
We sought a home where we uninjured might abide.

Can I forget that miserable hour,
When from the last hill-top, my sire surveyed,
Peering above the trees, the steeple tower,
That on his marriage-day sweet music made?
Till then he hoped his bones might there be laid,
Close by my mother in their native bowers: 60
Bidding me trust in God, he stood and prayed,—
I could not pray:—through tears that fell in showers,
Glimmer'd our dear-loved home, alas! no longer ours!

There was a youth whom I had loved so long,
That when I loved him not I cannot say.
'Mid the green mountains many and many a song
We two had sung, like little birds in May.
When we began to tire of childish play
We seemed still more and more to prize each other:

---

* Several of the Lakes in the north of England are let out to different Fishermen, in parcels marked out by imaginary lines drawn from rock to rock.

We talked of marriage and our marriage day; 70
And I in truth did love him like a brother,
For never could I hope to meet with such another.

His father said, that to a distant town
He must repair, to ply the artist's trade.
What tears of bitter grief till then unknown!
What tender vows our last sad kiss delayed!
To him we turned:—we had no other aid.
Like one revived, upon his neck I wept,
And her whom he had loved in joy, he said
He well could love in grief: his faith he kept; 80
And in a quiet home once more my father slept.

Four years each day with daily bread was blest,
By constant toil and constant prayer supplied.
Three lovely infants lay upon my breast;
And often, viewing their sweet smiles, I sighed,
And knew not why. My happy father died
When sad distress reduced the children's meal:
Thrice happy! that from him the grave did hide
The empty loom, cold hearth, and silent wheel,
And tears that flowed for ills which patience could not heal. 90

'Twas a hard change, an evil time was come;
We had no hope, and no relief could gain.
But soon, with proud parade, the noisy drum
Beat round, to sweep the streets of want and pain.
My husband's arms now only served to strain
Me and his children hungering in his view:
In such dismay my prayers and tears were vain:
To join those miserable men he flew;
And now to the sea-coast, with numbers more, we drew.

THE FEMALE VAGRANT

There foul neglect for months and months we bore,   100
Nor yet the crowded fleet its anchor stirred.
Green fields before us and our native shore,
By fever, from polluted air incurred,
Ravage was made, for which no knell was heard.
Fondly we wished, and wished away, nor knew,
'Mid that long sickness, and those hopes deferr'd,
That happier days we never more must view:
The parting signal streamed, at last the land withdrew,

But from delay the summer calms were past.
On as we drove, the equinoctial deep   110
Ran mountains-high before the howling blast.
We gazed with terror on the gloomy sleep
Of them that perished in the whirlwind's sweep,
Untaught that soon such anguish must ensue,
Our hopes such harvest of affliction reap,
That we the mercy of the waves should rue.
We reached the western world, a poor, devoted crew.

Oh! dreadful price of being to resign
All that is dear *in* being! better far
In Want's most lonely cave till death to pine,   120
Unseen, unheard, unwatched by any star;
Or in the streets and walks where proud men are,
Better our dying bodies to obtrude,
Than dog-like, wading at the heels of war,
Protract a curst existence, with the brood
That lap (their very nourishment!) their brother's blood.

The pains and plagues that on our heads came down,
Disease and famine, agony and fear,
In wood or wilderness, in camp or town,

It would thy brain unsettle even to hear. 130
All perished—all, in one remorseless year,
Husband and children! one by one, by sword
And ravenous plague, all perished: every tear
Dried up, despairing, desolate, on board
A British ship I waked, as from a trance restored.

Peaceful as some immeasurable plain
By the first beams of dawning light impress'd,
In the calm sunshine slept the glittering main.
The very ocean has its hour of rest,
That comes not to the human mourner's breast. 140
Remote from man, and storms of mortal care,
A heavenly silence did the waves invest;
I looked and looked along the silent air,
Until it seemed to bring a joy to my despair.

Ah! how unlike those late terrific sleeps!
And groans, that rage of racking famine spoke,
Where looks inhuman dwelt on festering heaps!
The breathing pestilence that rose like smoke!
The shriek that from the distant battle broke!
The mine's dire earthquake, and the pallid host 150
Driven by the bomb's incessant thunder-stroke
To loathsome vaults, where heart-sick anguish toss'd,
Hope died, and fear itself in agony was lost!

Yet does that burst of woe congeal my frame,
When the dark streets appeared to heave and gape,
While like a sea the storming army came,
And Fire from Hell reared his gigantic shape,
And Murder, by the ghastly gleam, and Rape
Seized their joint prey, the mother and the child!

But from these crazing thoughts my brain, escape! 160
—For weeks the balmy air breathed soft and mild,
And on the gliding vessel Heaven and Ocean smiled.

Some mighty gulph of separation past,
I seemed transported to another world:—
A thought resigned with pain, when from the mast
The impatient mariner the sail unfurl'd,
And whistling, called the wind that hardly curled
The silent sea. From the sweet thoughts of home,
And from all hope I was forever hurled.
For me—farthest from earthly port to roam 170
Was best, could I but shun the spot where man might come.

And oft, robb'd of my perfect mind, I thought
At last my feet a resting-place had found:
Here will I weep in peace, (so fancy wrought,)
Roaming the illimitable waters round;
Here watch, of every human friend disowned,
All day, my ready tomb the ocean-flood—
To break my dream the vessel reached its bound:
And homeless near a thousand homes I stood,
And near a thousand tables pined, and wanted food. 180

By grief enfeebled was I turned adrift,
Helpless as sailor cast on desart rock;
Nor morsel to my mouth that day did lift,
Nor dared my hand at any door to knock.
I lay, where with his drowsy mates, the cock
From the cross timber of an out-house hung;
How dismal tolled, that night, the city clock!
At morn my sick heart hunger scarcely stung,
Nor to the beggar's language could I frame my tongue.

So passed another day, and so the third: 190
Then did I try, in vain, the crowd's resort,
In deep despair by frightful wishes stirr'd,
Near the sea-side I reached a ruined fort:
There, pains which nature could no more support,
With blindness linked, did on my vitals fall;
Dizzy my brain, with interruption short
Of hideous sense; I sunk, nor step could crawl,
And thence was borne away to neighbouring hospital.

Recovery came with food: but still, my brain
Was weak, nor of the past had memory. 200
I heard my neighbours, in their beds, complain
Of many things which never troubled me;
Of feet still bustling round with busy glee,
Of looks where common kindness had no part,
Of service done with careless cruelty,
Fretting the fever round the languid heart,
And groans, which, as they said, would make a dead man start.

These things just served to stir the torpid sense,
Nor pain nor pity in my bosom raised.
Memory, though slow, returned with strength; and thence
Dismissed, again on open day I gazed, 211
At houses, men, and common light, amazed.
The lanes I sought, and as the sun retired,
Came, where beneath the trees a faggot blazed;
The wild brood saw me weep, my fate enquired,
And gave me food, and rest, more welcome, more desired.

My heart is touched to think that men like these,
The rude earth's tenants, were my first relief:
How kindly did they paint their vagrant ease!

THE FEMALE VAGRANT

And their long holiday that feared not grief, 220
For all belonged to all, and each was chief.
No plough their sinews strained; on grating road
No wain they drove, and yet, the yellow sheaf
In every vale for their delight was stowed:
For them, in nature's meads, the milky udder flowed.

Semblance, with straw and panniered ass, they made
Of potters wandering on from door to door:
But life of happier sort to me pourtrayed,
And other joys my fancy to allure;
The bag-pipe dinning on the midnight moor 230
In barn uplighted, and companions boon
Well met from far with revelry secure,
In depth of forest glade, when jocund June
Rolled fast along the sky his warm and genial moon.

But ill it suited me, in journey dark
O'er moor and mountain, midnight theft to hatch;
To charm the surly house-dog's faithful bark,
Or hang on tiptoe at the lifted latch;
The gloomy lantern, and the dim blue match,
The black disguise, the warning whistle shrill, 240
And ear still busy on its nightly watch,
Were not for me, brought up in nothing ill;
Besides, on griefs so fresh my thoughts were brooding still.

What could I do, unaided and unblest?
Poor Father! gone was every friend of thine:
And kindred of dead husband are at best
Small help, and, after marriage such as mine,
With little kindness would to me incline.
Ill was I then for toil or service fit:

With tears whose course no effort could confine, 250
By high-way side forgetful would I sit
Whole hours, my idle arms in moping sorrow knit.

I lived upon the mercy of the fields,
And oft of cruelty the sky accused;
On hazard, or what general bounty yields,
Now coldly given, now utterly refused.
The fields I for my bed have often used:
But, what afflicts my peace with keenest ruth
Is, that I have my inner self abused,
Foregone the home delight of constant truth, 260
And clear and open soul, so prized in fearless youth.

Three years a wanderer, often have I view'd,
In tears, the sun towards that country tend
Where my poor heart lost all its fortitude:
And now across this moor my steps I bend—
Oh! tell me whither——for no earthly friend
Have I.——She ceased, and weeping turned away,
As if because her tale was at an end
She wept;—because she had no more to say
Of that perpetual weight which on her spirit lay. 270

Goody Blake and Harry Gill

A TRUE STORY

Oh! what's the matter? what's the matter?
What is't that ails young Harry Gill?
That evermore his teeth they chatter,
Chatter, chatter, chatter still.

GOODY BLAKE AND HARRY GILL

Of waistcoats Harry has no lack,
Good duffle grey, and flannel fine;
He has a blanket on his back,
And coats enough to smother nine.

In March, December, and in July,
'Tis all the same with Harry Gill;
The neighbours tell, and tell you truly,
His teeth they chatter, chatter still.
At night, at morning, and at noon,
'Tis all the same with Harry Gill;
Beneath the sun, beneath the moon,
His teeth they chatter, chatter still.

Young Harry was a lusty drover,
And who so stout of limb as he?
His cheeks were red as ruddy clover,
His voice was like the voice of three.
Auld Goody Blake was old and poor,
Ill fed she was, and thinly clad;
And any man who pass'd her door,
Might see how poor a hut she had.

All day she spun in her poor dwelling,
And then her three hours' work at night!
Alas! 'twas hardly worth the telling,
It would not pay for candle-light.
—This woman dwelt in Dorsetshire,
Her hut was on a cold hill-side,
And in that country coals are dear,
For they come far by wind and tide.

GOODY BLAKE AND HARRY GILL

By the same fire to boil their pottage,
Two poor old dames, as I have known,
Will often live in one small cottage,
But she, poor woman, dwelt alone.
'Twas well enough when summer came,
The long, warm, lightsome summer-day,
Then at her door the *canty* dame
Would sit, as any linnet gay. 40

But when the ice our streams did fetter,
Oh! then how her old bones would shake!
You would have said, if you had met her,
'Twas a hard time for Goody Blake.
Her evenings then were dull and dead;
Sad case it was, as you may think,
For very cold to go to bed,
And then for cold not sleep a wink.

Oh joy for her! when e'er in winter
The winds at night had made a rout, 50
And scatter'd many a lusty splinter,
And many a rotten bough about.
Yet never had she, well or sick,
As every man who knew her says,
A pile before-hand, wood or stick,
Enough to warm her for three days.

Now, when the frost was past enduring,
And made her poor old bones to ache,
Could any thing be more alluring,
Than an old hedge to Goody Blake? 60
And now and then, it must be said,
When her old bones were cold and chill,

GOODY BLAKE AND HARRY GILL

She left her fire, or left her bed,
To seek the hedge of Harry Gill.

Now Harry he had long suspected
This trespass of old Goody Blake,
And vow'd that she should be detected,
And he on her would vengeance take.
And oft from his warm fire he'd go,
And to the fields his road would take,
And there, at night, in frost and snow,
He watch'd to seize old Goody Blake.

And once, behind a rick of barley,
Thus looking out did Harry stand;
The moon was full and shining clearly,
And crisp with frost the stubble-land.
—He hears a noise—he's all awake—
Again?—on tip-toe down the hill
He softly creeps—'Tis Goody Blake,
She's at the hedge of Harry Gill.

Right glad was he when he beheld her:
Stick after stick did Goody pull,
He stood behind a bush of elder,
Till she had filled her apron full.
When with her load she turned about,
The bye-road back again to take,
He started forward with a shout,
And sprang upon poor Goody Blake.

And fiercely by the arm he took her,
And by the arm he held her fast,
And fiercely by the arm he shook her,

GOODY BLAKE AND HARRY GILL

And cried, 'I've caught you then at last!'
Then Goody, who had nothing said,
Her bundle from her lap let fall;
And kneeling on the sticks, she pray'd
To God that is the judge of all.

She pray'd, her wither'd hand uprearing,
While Harry held her by the arm—
'God! who art never out of hearing,
'O may he never more be warm!'   100
The cold, cold moon above her head,
Thus on her knees did Goody pray,
Young Harry heard what she had said,
And icy-cold he turned away.

He went complaining all the morrow
That he was cold and very chill:
His face was gloom, his heart was sorrow,
Alas! that day for Harry Gill!
That day he wore a riding-coat,
But not a whit the warmer he: 110
Another was on Thursday brought,
And ere the Sabbath he had three.

'Twas all in vain, a useless matter,
And blankets were about him pinn'd;
Yet still his jaws and teeth they clatter,
Like a loose casement in the wind.
And Harry's flesh it fell away;
And all who see him say 'tis plain,
That, live as long as live he may,
He never will be warm again.   120

No word to any man he utters,
A-bed or up, to young or old;
But ever to himself he mutters,
'Poor Harry Gill is very cold.'
A-bed or up, by night or day;
His teeth they chatter, chatter still.
Now think, ye farmers all, I pray,
Of Goody Blake and Harry Gill.

Lines

WRITTEN AT A SMALL DISTANCE FROM MY HOUSE, AND SENT BY MY LITTLE BOY TO THE PERSON TO WHOM THEY ARE ADDRESSED

It is the first mild day of March:
Each minute sweeter than before,
The red-breast sings from the tall larch
That stands beside our door.

There is a blessing in the air,
Which seems a sense of joy to yield
To the bare trees, and mountains bare,
And grass in the green field.

My Sister! ('tis a wish of mine)
Now that our morning meal is done,
Make haste, your morning task resign;
Come forth and feel the sun.

10

Edward will come with you, and pray,
Put on with speed your woodland dress,
And bring no book, for this one day
We'll give to idleness.

No joyless forms shall regulate
Our living Calendar:
We from to-day, my friend, will date
The opening of the year.

Love, now an universal birth,
From heart to heart is stealing,
From earth to man, from man to earth,
—It is the hour of feeling.

One moment now may give us more
Than fifty years of reason;
Our minds shall drink at every pore
The spirit of the season.

Some silent laws our hearts may make,
Which they shall long obey;
We for the year to come may take
Our temper from to-day.

And from the blessed power that rolls
About, below, above;
We'll frame the measure of our souls,
They shall be tuned to love.

Then come, my sister! come, I pray,
With speed put on your woodland dress,
And bring no book; for this one day
We'll give to idleness.

Simon Lee, the Old Huntsman

WITH AN INCIDENT IN WHICH HE WAS CONCERNED

> In the sweet shire of Cardigan,
> Not far from pleasant Ivor-hall,
> An old man dwells, a little man,
> I've heard he once was tall.
> Of years he has upon his back,
> No doubt, a burthen weighty;
> He says he is three score and ten,
> But others say he's eighty.
>
> A long blue livery-coat has he,
> That's fair behind, and fair before;
> Yet, meet him where you will, you see
> At once that he is poor.
> Full five and twenty years he lived
> A running huntsman merry;
> And, though he has but one eye left,
> His cheek is like a cherry.
>
> No man like him the horn could sound,
> And no man was so full of glee;
> To say the least, four counties round
> Had heard of Simon Lee;
> His master's dead, and no one now
> Dwells in the hall of Ivor;
> Men, dogs, and horses, all are dead;
> He is the sole survivor.

SIMON LEE, THE OLD HUNTSMAN

His hunting feats have him bereft
Of his right eye, as you may see:
And then, what limbs those feats have left
To poor old Simon Lee!
He has no son, he has no child,
His wife, an aged woman, 30
Lives with him, near the waterfall,
Upon the village common.

And he is lean and he is sick,
His little body's half awry
His ancles they are swoln and thick;
His legs are thin and dry.
When he was young he little knew
Of husbandry or tillage;
And now he's forced to work, though weak,
—The weakest in the village. 40

He all the country could outrun,
Could leave both man and horse behind;
And often, ere the race was done,
He reeled and was stone-blind.
And still there's something in the world
At which his heart rejoices;
For when the chiming hounds are out,
He dearly loves their voices!

Old Ruth works out of doors with him,
And does what Simon cannot do; 50
For she, not over stout of limb,
Is stouter of the two.
And though you with your utmost skill
From labour could not wean them,

SIMON LEE, THE OLD HUNTSMAN

Alas! 'tis very little, all
Which they can do between them.

Beside their moss-grown hut of clay,
Not twenty paces from the door,
A scrap of land they have, but they
Are poorest of the poor.
This scrap of land he from the heath
Enclosed when he was stronger;
But what avails the land to them,
Which they can till no longer?

Few months of life has he in store,
As he to you will tell,
For still, the more he works, the more
His poor old ancles swell.
My gentle reader, I perceive
How patiently you've waited,
And I'm afraid that you expect
Some tale will be related.

O reader! had you in your mind
Such stores as silent thought can bring,
O gentle reader! you would find
A tale in every thing.
What more I have to say is short,
I hope you'll kindly take it;
It is no tale; but should you think,
Perhaps a tale you'll make it.

One summer-day I chanced to see
This old man doing all he could
About the root of an old tree,

A stump of rotten wood.
The mattock totter'd in his hand;
So vain was his endeavour
That at the root of the old tree
He might have worked for ever.

'You're overtasked, good Simon Lee,
Give me your tool' to him I said;   90
And at the word right gladly he
Received my proffer'd aid.
I struck, and with a single blow
The tangled root I sever'd,
At which the poor old man so long
And vainly had endeavour'd.

The tears into his eyes were brought,
And thanks and praises seemed to run
So fast out of his heart, I thought
They never would have done.   100
—I've heard of hearts unkind, kind deeds
With coldness still returning.
Alas! the gratitude of men
Has oftner left me mourning.

Anecdote for Fathers,

SHEWING HOW THE ART OF LYING MAY BE TAUGHT

I have a boy of five years old,
His face is fair and fresh to see;
His limbs are cast in beauty's mould,
And dearly he loves me.

ANECDOTE FOR FATHERS

One morn we stroll'd on our dry walk,
Our quiet house all full in view,
And held such intermitted talk
As we are wont to do.

My thoughts on former pleasures ran;
I thought of Kilve's delightful shore,
My pleasant home, when spring began,
A long, long year before.

A day it was when I could bear
To think, and think, and think again;
With so much happiness to spare,
I could not feel a pain.

My boy was by my side, so slim
And graceful in his rustic dress!
And oftentimes I talked to him,
In very idleness.

The young lambs ran a pretty race;
The morning sun shone bright and warm;
'Kilve,' said I, 'was a pleasant place,
'And so is Liswyn farm.

'My little boy, which like you more,'
I said and took him by the arm—
'Our home by Kilve's delightful shore,
'Or here at Liswyn farm?'

'And tell me, had you rather be,'
I said and held him by the arm,

'At Kilve's smooth shore by the green sea,
'Or here at Liswyn farm?

In careless mood he looked at me,
While still I held him by the arm,
And said, 'At Kilve I'd rather be
'Than here at Liswyn farm.'

'Now, little Edward, say why so;
My little Edward, tell me why;'
'I cannot tell, I do not know.'
'Why this is strange,' said I. 40

'For, here are woods and green-hills warm;
'There surely must some reason be
'Why you would change sweet Liswyn farm
'For Kilve by the green sea.'

At this, my boy, so fair and slim,
Hung down his head, nor made reply;
And five times did I say to him,
'Why? Edward, tell me why?'

His head he raised—there was in sight,
It caught his eye, he saw it plain— 50
Upon the house-top, glittering bright,
A broad and gilded vane.

Then did the boy his tongue unlock,
And thus to me he made reply;
'At Kilve there was no weather-cock,
'And that's the reason why.'

O dearest, dearest boy! my heart
For better lore would seldom yearn,
Could I but teach the hundredth part
Of what from thee I learn.

We Are Seven

A simple child, dear brother Jim,
That lightly draws its breath,
And feels its life in every limb,
What should it know of death?

I met a little cottage girl,
She was eight years old, she said;
Her hair was thick with many a curl
That cluster'd round her head.

She had a rustic, woodland air,
And she was wildly clad;
Her eyes were fair, and very fair,
—Her beauty made me glad.

'Sisters and brothers, little maid,
'How many may you be?'
'How many? seven in all,' she said,
And wondering looked at me.

'And where are they, I pray you tell?'
She answered, 'Seven are we,
'And two of us at Conway dwell,
'And two are gone to sea.

'Two of us in the church-yard lie,
'My sister and my brother,
'And in the church-yard cottage, I
'Dwell near them with my mother.'

'You say that two at Conway dwell,
'And two are gone to sea,
'Yet you are seven; I pray you tell
'Sweet Maid, how this may be?'

Then did the little Maid reply,
'Seven boys and girls are we;
'Two of us in the church-yard lie,
'Beneath the church-yard tree.'

'You run about, my little maid,
'Your limbs they are alive;
'If two are in the church-yard laid,
'Then ye are only five.'

'Their graves are green, they may be seen,'
The little Maid replied,
'Twelve steps or more from my mother's door,
'And they are side by side.

'My stockings there I often knit,
'My 'kerchief there I hem;
'And there upon the ground I sit—
'I sit and sing to them.

'And often after sunset, Sir,
'When it is light and fair,
'I take my little porringer,
'And eat my supper there.

'The first that died was little Jane;
'In bed she moaning lay, 50
'Till God released her of her pain,
'And then she went away.

'So in the church-yard she was laid,
'And all the summer dry,
'Together round her grave we played,
'My brother John and I.

'And when the ground was white with snow,
'And I could run and slide,
'My brother John was forced to go,
'And he lies by her side.' 60

'How many are you then,' said I,
'If they two are in Heaven?'
The little Maiden did reply,
'O Master! we are seven.'

'But they are dead; those two are dead!
'Their spirits are in heaven!'
'Twas throwing words away; for still
The little Maid would have her will,
And said, 'Nay, we are seven!'

Lines written in Early Spring

I heard a thousand blended notes,
While in a grove I sate reclined,
In that sweet mood when pleasant thoughts
Bring sad thoughts to the mind.

LINES WRITTEN IN EARLY SPRING

To her fair works did nature link
The human soul that through me ran;
And much it griev'd my heart to think
What man has made of man.

Through primrose-tufts, in that sweet bower,
The periwinkle trail'd its wreathes;   10
And 'tis my faith that every flower
Enjoys the air it breathes.

The birds around me hopp'd and play'd:
Their thoughts I cannot measure,
But the least motion which they made,
It seem'd a thrill of pleasure.

The budding twigs spread out their fan,
To catch the breezy air;
And I must think, do all I can,
That there was pleasure there.   20

If I these thoughts may not prevent,
If such be of my creed the plan,
Have I not reason to lament
What man has made of man?

The Thorn

I

There is a thorn; it looks so old,
In truth you'd find it hard to say,
How it could ever have been young,

It looks so old and grey.
Not higher than a two-years' child,
It stands erect this aged thorn;
No leaves it has, no thorny points;
It is a mass of knotted joints,
A wretched thing forlorn.
It stands erect, and like a stone
With lichens it is overgrown.

II

Like rock or stone, it is o'ergrown
With lichens to the very top,
And hung with heavy tufts of moss,
A melancholy crop:
Up from the earth these mosses creep,
And this poor thorn they clasp it round
So close, you'd say that they were bent
With plain and manifest intent,
To drag it to the ground;
And all had joined in one endeavour
To bury this poor thorn for ever.

III

High on a mountain's highest ridge,
Where oft the stormy winter gale
Cuts like a scythe, while through the clouds
It sweeps from vale to vale;
Not five yards from the mountain-path,
This thorn you on your left espy;
And to the left, three yards beyond,
You see a little muddy pond

Of water, never dry;
I've measured it from side to side:
'Tis three feet long, and two feet wide.

IV

And close beside this aged thorn,
There is a fresh and lovely sight,
A beauteous heap, a hill of moss,
Just half a foot in height.
All lovely colours there you see,
All colours that were ever seen,
And mossy network too is there, 40
As if by hand of lady fair
The work had woven been,
And cups, the darlings of the eye,
So deep is their vermilion dye.

V

Ah me! what lovely tints are there!
Of olive-green and scarlet bright,
In spikes, in branches, and in stars,
Green, red, and pearly white.
This heap of earth o'ergrown with moss,
Which close beside the thorn you see, 50
So fresh in all its beauteous dyes,
Is like an infant's grave in size
As like as like can be:
But never, never any where,
An infant's grave was half so fair.

VI

Now would you see this aged thorn,
This pond and beauteous hill of moss,
You must take care and chuse your time
The mountain when to cross.
For oft there sits, between the heap
That's like an infant's grave in size,
And that same pond of which I spoke,
A woman in a scarlet cloak,
And to herself she cries,
'Oh misery! oh misery!
'Oh woe is me! oh misery!'

VII

At all times of the day and night
This wretched woman thither goes,
And she is known to every star,
And every wind that blows;
And there beside the thorn she sits
When the blue day-light's in the skies,
And when the whirlwind's on the hill,
Or frosty air is keen and still,
And to herself she cries,
'Oh misery! oh misery!
'Oh woe is me! oh misery!'

VIII

'Now wherefore thus, by day and night,
'In rain, in tempest, and in snow,

THE THORN

'Thus to the dreary mountain-top
'Does this poor woman go?
'And why sits she beside the thorn
'When the blue day-light's in the sky,
'Or when the whirlwind's on the hill,
'Or frosty air is keen and still,
'And wherefore does she cry?—
'Oh wherefore? wherefore? tell me why
'Does she repeat that doleful cry?'

IX

I cannot tell; I wish I could;
For the true reason no one knows,
But if you'd gladly view the spot,
The spot to which she goes;
The heap that's like an infant's grave,
The pond—and thorn, so old and grey,
Pass by her door—tis seldom shut—
And if you see her in her hut,
Then to the spot away!—
I never heard of such as dare
Approach the spot when she is there.

X

'But wherefore to the mountain-top
'Can this unhappy woman go,
'Whatever star is in the skies,
'Whatever wind may blow?'
Nay rack your brain—'tis all in vain,
I'll tell you every thing I know;
But to the thorn, and to the pond

Which is a little step beyond,
I wish that you would go:
Perhaps when you are at the place
You something of her tale may trace.

XI

I'll give you the best help I can:
Before you up the mountain go,
Up to the dreary mountain-top,
I'll tell you all I know.
'Tis now some two and twenty years,
Since she (her name is Martha Ray)
Gave with a maiden's true good will
Her company to Stephen Hill;
And she was blithe and gay,
And she was happy, happy still
Whene'er she thought of Stephen Hill.

XII

And they had fix'd the wedding-day,
The morning that must wed them both;
But Stephen to another maid
Had sworn another oath;
And with this other maid to church
Unthinking Stephen went—
Poor Martha! on that woful day
A cruel, cruel fire, they say,
Into her bones was sent:
It dried her body like a cinder,
And almost turn'd her brain to tinder.

XIII

They say, full six months after this,
While yet the summer-leaves were green,
She to the mountain-top would go,
And there was often seen.
'Tis said, a child was in her womb,
As now to any eye was plain;
She was with child, and she was mad,
Yet often she was sober sad 140
From her exceeding pain.
Oh me! ten thousand times I'd rather
That he had died, that cruel father!

XIV

Sad case for such a brain to hold
Communion with a stirring child!
Sad case, as you may think, for one
Who had a brain so wild!
Last Christmas when we talked of this,
Old Farmer Simpson did maintain,
That in her womb the infant wrought 150
About its mother's heart, and brought
Her senses back again:
And when at last her time drew near,
Her looks were calm, her senses clear.

XV

No more I know, I wish I did,
And I would tell it all to you;

THE THORN

For what became of this poor child
There's none that ever knew:
And if a child was born or no,
There's no one that could ever tell;
And if 'twas born alive or dead,
There's no one knows, as I have said,
But some remember well,
That Martha Ray about this time
Would up the mountain often climb.

XVI

And all that winter, when at night
The wind blew from the mountain-peak,
'Twas worth your while, though in the dark,
The church-yard path to seek:
For many a time and oft were heard
Cries coming from the mountain-head,
Some plainly living voices were,
And others, I've heard many swear,
Were voices of the dead:
I cannot think, whate'er they say,
They had to do with Martha Ray.

XVII

But that she goes to this old thorn,
The thorn which I've described to you,
And there sits in a scarlet cloak,
I will be sworn is true.
For one day with my telescope,
To view the ocean wide and bright,
When to this country first I came,

Ere I had heard of Martha's name,
I climbed the mountain's height:
A storm came on, and I could see
No object higher than my knee.

XVIII

'Twas mist and rain, and storm and rain,
No screen, no fence could I discover,
And then the wind! in faith, it was 190
A wind full ten times over.
I looked around, I thought I saw
A jutting crag, and off I ran,
Head-foremost, through the driving rain,
The shelter of the crag to gain,
And, as I am a man,
Instead of jutting crag, I found
A woman seated on the ground.

XIX

I did not speak—I saw her face,
Her face it was enough for me; 200
I turned about and heard her cry,
'O misery! O misery!'
And there she sits, until the moon
Through half the clear blue sky will go,
And when the little breezes make
The waters of the pond to shake,
As all the country know,
She shudders and you hear her cry,
'Oh misery! oh misery!

XX

'But what's the thorn? and what's the pond? 210
'And what's the hill of moss to her?
'And what's the creeping breeze that comes
'The little pond to stir?'
I cannot tell; but some will say
She hanged her baby on the tree,
Some say she drowned it in the pond,
Which is a little step beyond,
But all and each agree,
The little babe was buried there,
Beneath that hill of moss so fair. 220

XXI

I've heard the scarlet moss is red
With drops of that poor infant's blood;
But kill a new-born infant thus!
I do not think she could.
Some say, if to the pond you go,
And fix on it a steady view,
The shadow of a babe you trace,
A baby and a baby's face,
And that it looks at you;
Whene'er you look on it, 'tis plain 230
The baby looks at you again.

XXII

And some had sworn an oath that she
Should be to public justice brought;

And for the little infant's bones
With spades they would have sought.
But then the beauteous hill of moss
Before their eyes began to stir;
And for full fifty yards around,
The grass it shook upon the ground;
But all do still aver 240
The little babe is buried there,
Beneath that hill of moss so fair.

XXIII

I cannot tell how this may be,
But plain it is, the thorn is bound
With heavy tufts of moss, that strive
To drag it to the ground.
And this I know, full many a time,
When she was on the mountain high,
By day, and in the silent night,
When all the stars shone clear and bright, 250
That I have heard her cry,
'Oh misery! oh misery!
'O woe is me! oh misery!'

The Last of the Flock

In distant countries I have been,
And yet I have not often seen
A healthy man, a man full grown,
Weep in the public roads alone.
But such a one, on English ground,
And in the broad high-way, I met;

THE LAST OF THE FLOCK

Along the broad high-way he came,
His cheeks with tears were wet.
Sturdy he seemed, though he was sad;
And in his arms a lamb he had.   10

He saw me, and he turned aside,
As if he wished himself to hide:
Then with his coat he made essay
To wipe those briny tears away.
I follow'd him, and said, 'My friend
'What ails you? wherefore weep you so?'
—'Shame on me, Sir! this lusty lamb,
He makes my tears to flow.
To-day I fetched him from the rock;
He is the last of all my flock.   20

When I was young, a single man,
And after youthful follies ran,
Though little given to care and thought,
Yet, so it was, a ewe I bought;
And other sheep from her I raised,
As healthy sheep as you might see,
And then I married, and was rich
As I could wish to be;
Of sheep I number'd a full score,
And every year encreas'd my store.   30

Year after year my stock it grew,
And from this one, this single ewe,
Full fifty comely sheep I raised,
As sweet a flock as ever grazed!
Upon the mountain did they feed;
They throve, and we at home did thrive.

THE LAST OF THE FLOCK

—This lusty lamb of all my store
Is all that is alive:
And now I care not if we die,
And perish all of poverty. 40

Ten children, Sir! had I to feed,
Hard labour in a time of need!
My pride was tamed, and in our grief
I of the parish ask'd relief.
They said I was a wealthy man;
My sheep upon the mountain fed,
And it was fit that thence I took
Whereof to buy us bread:'
'Do this; how can we give to you,'
They cried, 'what to the poor is due?' 50

I sold a sheep as they had said,
And bought my little children bread,
And they were healthy with their food;
For me it never did me good.
A woeful time it was for me,
To see the end of all my gains,
The pretty flock which I had reared
With all my care and pains,
To see it melt like snow away!
For me it was a woeful day. 60

Another still! and still another!
A little lamb, and then its mother!
It was a vein that never stopp'd,
Like blood-drops from my heart they dropp'd.
Till thirty were not left alive
They dwindled, dwindled, one by one,

THE LAST OF THE FLOCK

And I may say that many a time
I wished they all were gone:
They dwindled one by one away;
For me it was a woeful day. 70

To wicked deeds I was inclined,
And wicked fancies cross'd my mind,
And every man I chanc'd to see,
I thought he knew some ill of me.
No peace, no comfort could I find,
No ease, within doors or without,
And crazily, and wearily,
I went my work about.
Oft-times I thought to run away;
For me it was a woeful day. 80

Sir! 'twas a precious flock to me,
As dear as my own children be;
For daily with my growing store
I loved my children more and more.
Alas! it was an evil time;
God cursed me in my sore distress,
I prayed, yet every day I thought
I loved my children less;
And every week, and every day,
My flock, it seemed to melt away. 90

They dwindled, Sir, sad sight to see!
From ten to five, from five to three,
A lamb, a weather, and a ewe;
And then at last, from three to two;
And of my fifty, yesterday
I had but only one,

And here it lies upon my arm,
Alas! and I have none;
To-day I fetched it from the rock;
It is the last of all my flock.' 100

The Dungeon

And this place our forefathers made for man!
This is the process of our love and wisdom,
To each poor brother who offends against us—
Most innocent, perhaps—and what if guilty?
Is this the only cure? Merciful God!
Each pore and natural outlet shrivell'd up
By ignorance and parching poverty,
His energies roll back upon his heart,
And stagnate and corrupt; till changed to poison, 9
They break out on him, like a loathsome plague-spot;
Then we call in our pamper'd mountebanks—
And this is their best cure! uncomforted
And friendless solitude, groaning and tears,
And savage faces, at the clanking hour,
Seen through the steams and vapour of his dungeon,
By the lamp's dismal twilight! So he lies
Circled with evil, till his very soul
Unmoulds its essence, hopelessly deformed
By sights of ever more deformity!

With other ministrations thou, O nature! 20
Healest thy wandering and distempered child:
Thou pourest on him thy soft influences,
Thy sunny hues, fair forms, and breathing sweets,

Thy melodies of woods, and winds, and waters,
Till he relent, and can no more endure
To be a jarring and a dissonant thing,
Amid this general dance and minstrelsy;
But, bursting into tears, wins back his way,
His angry spirit healed and harmonized
By the benignant touch of love and beauty.   30

The Mad Mother

Her eyes are wild, her head is bare,
The sun has burnt her coal-black hair,
Her eye-brows have a rusty stain,
And she came far from over the main.
She has a baby on her arm,
Or else she were alone;
And underneath the hay-stack warm,
And on the green-wood stone,
She talked and sung the woods among;
And it was in the English tongue.   10

'Sweet babe! they say that I am mad,
But nay, my heart is far too glad;
And I am happy when I sing
Full many a sad and doleful thing:
Then, lovely baby, do not fear!
I pray thee have no fear of me,
But, safe as in a cradle, here
My lovely baby! thou shalt be,
To thee I know too much I owe;
I cannot work thee any woe.   20

THE MAD MOTHER

A fire was once within my brain;
And in my head a dull, dull pain;
And fiendish faces one, two, three,
Hung at my breasts, and pulled at me.
But then there came a sight of joy;
It came at once to do me good;
I waked, and saw my little boy,
My little boy of flesh and blood;
Oh joy for me that sight to see!
For he was here, and only he. 30

Suck, little babe, oh suck again!
It cools my blood; it cools my brain;
Thy lips I feel them, baby! they
Draw from my heart the pain away.
Oh! press me with thy little hand;
It loosens something at my chest;
About that tight and deadly band
I feel thy little fingers press'd.
The breeze I see is in the tree;
It comes to cool my babe and me. 40

Oh! love me, love me, little boy!
Thou art thy mother's only joy;
And do not dread the waves below,
When o'er the sea-rock's edge we go;
The high crag cannot work me harm,
Nor leaping torrents when they howl;
The babe I carry on my arm,
He saves for me my precious soul;
Then happy lie, for blest am I;
Without me my sweet babe would die. 50

THE MAD MOTHER

Then do not fear, my boy! for thee
Bold as a lion I will be;
And I will always be thy guide,
Through hollow snows and rivers wide.
I'll build an Indian bower; I know
The leaves that make the softest bed:
And if from me thou wilt not go,
But still be true 'till I am dead,
My pretty thing! then thou shalt sing,
As merry as the birds in spring.   60

Thy father cares not for my breast,
'Tis thine, sweet baby, there to rest:
'Tis all thine own! and if its hue
Be changed, that was so fair to view,
'Tis fair enough for thee, my dove!
My beauty, little child, is flown;
But thou wilt live with me in love,
And what if my poor cheek be brown?
'Tis well for me; thou canst not see
How pale and wan it else would be.   70

Dread not their taunts, my little life!
I am thy father's wedded wife;
And underneath the spreading tree
We two will live in honesty.
If his sweet boy he could forsake,
With me he never would have stay'd:
From him no harm my babe can take,
But he, poor man! is wretched made,
And every day we two will pray
For him that's gone and far away.   80

I'll teach my boy the sweetest things;
I'll teach him how the owlet sings.
My little babe! thy lips are still,
And thou hast almost suck'd thy fill.
—Where art thou gone my own dear child?
What wicked looks are those I see?
Alas! alas! that look so wild,
It never, never came from me:
If thou art mad, my pretty lad,
Then I must be for ever sad. 90

Oh! smile on me, my little lamb!
For I thy own dear mother am.
My love for thee has well been tried:
I've sought thy father far and wide.
I know the poisons of the shade,
I know the earth-nuts fit for food;
Then, pretty dear, be not afraid;
We'll find thy father in the wood.
Now laugh and be gay, to the woods away!
And there, my babe; we'll live for aye. 100

The Idiot Boy

'Tis eight o'clock,—a clear March night,
The moon is up—the sky is blue,
The owlet in the moonlight air,
He shouts from nobody knows where;
He lengthens out his lonely shout,
Halloo! halloo! a long halloo!

THE IDIOT BOY

—Why bustle thus about your door,
What means this bustle, Betty Foy?
Why are you in this mighty fret?
And why on horseback have you set
Him whom you love, your idiot boy?

Beneath the moon that shines so bright,
Till she is tired, let Betty Foy
With girt and stirrup fiddle-faddle;
But wherefore set upon a saddle
Him whom she loves, her idiot boy?

There's scarce a soul that's out of bed;
Good Betty! put him down again;
His lips with joy they burr at you,
But, Betty! what has he to do
With stirrup, saddle, or with rein?

The world will say 'tis very idle,
Bethink you of the time of night;
There's not a mother, no not one,
But when she hears what you have done,
Oh! Betty she'll be in a fright.

But Betty's bent on her intent,
For her good neighbour, Susan Gale,
Old Susan, she who dwells alone,
Is sick, and makes a piteous moan,
As if her very life would fail.

There's not a house within a mile,
No hand to help them in distress:
Old Susan lies a bed in pain,

THE IDIOT BOY

And sorely puzzled are the twain,
For what she ails they cannot guess.

And Betty's husband's at the wood,
Where by the week he doth abide,
A woodman in the distant vale;
There's none to help poor Susan Gale,
What must be done? what will betide?

And Betty from the lane has fetched
Her pony, that is mild and good,
Whether he be in joy or pain,
Feeding at will along the lane,
Or bringing faggots from the wood.

And he is all in travelling trim,
And by the moonlight, Betty Foy
Has up upon the saddle set,
The like was never heard of yet,
Him whom she loves, her idiot boy.

And he must post without delay
Across the bridge that's in the dale,
And by the church, and o'er the down,
To bring a doctor from the town,
Or she will die, old Susan Gale.

There is no need of boot or spur,
There is no need of whip or wand,
For Johnny has his holly-bough,
And with a hurly-burly now
He shakes the green bough in his hand.

And Betty o'er and o'er has told
The boy who is her best delight,
Both what to follow, what to shun,
What do, and what to leave undone,
How turn to left, and how to right.

And Betty's most especial charge,
Was, 'Johnny! Johnny! mind that you
'Come home again, nor stop at all,
'Come home again, whate'er befal, 70
'My Johnny do, I pray you do.'

To this did Johnny answer make,
Both with his head, and with his hand,
And proudly shook the bridle too,
And then! his words were not a few,
Which Betty well could understand.

And now that Johnny is just going,
Though Betty's in a mighty flurry,
She gently pats the pony's side,
On which her idiot boy must ride, 80
And seems no longer in a hurry.

But when the pony moved his legs,
Oh! then for the poor idiot boy!
For joy he cannot hold the bridle,
For joy his head and heels are idle,
He's idle all for very joy.

And while the pony moves his legs,
In Johnny's left-hand you may see,
The green bough's motionless and dead;

THE IDIOT BOY

The moon that shines above his head 90
Is not more still and mute than he.

His heart it was so full of glee,
That till full fifty yards were gone,
He quite forgot his holly whip,
And all his skill in horsemanship,
Oh! happy, happy, happy John.

And Betty's standing at the door,
And Betty's face with joy o'erflows,
Proud of herself, and proud of him,
She sees him in his travelling trim; 100
How quietly her Johnny goes.

The silence of her idiot boy,
What hopes it sends to Betty's heart!
He's at the guide-post—he turns right,
She watches till he's out of sight,
And Betty will not then depart.

Burr, burr—now Johnny's lips they burr,
As loud as any mill, or near it,
Meek as a lamb the pony moves,
And Johnny makes the noise he loves, 110
And Betty listens, glad to hear it.

Away she hies to Susan Gale:
And Johnny's in a merry tune,
The owlets hoot, the owlets curr,
And Johnny's lips they burr, burr, burr,
And on he goes beneath the moon.

THE IDIOT BOY

His steed and he right well agree,
For of this pony there's a rumour,
That should he lose his eyes and ears,
And should he live a thousand years, 120
He never will be out of humour.

But then he is a horse that thinks!
And when he thinks his pace is slack;
Now, though he knows poor Johnny well,
Yet for his life he cannot tell
What he has got upon his back.

So through the moonlight lanes they go,
And far into the moonlight dale,
And by the church, and o'er the down,
To bring a doctor from the town, 130
To comfort poor old Susan Gale.

And Betty, now at Susan's side,
Is in the middle of her story,
What comfort Johnny soon will bring,
With many a most diverting thing,
Of Johnny's wit and Johnny's glory.

And Betty's still at Susan's side:
By this time she's not quite so flurried;
Demure with porringer and plate
She sits, as if in Susan's fate 140
Her life and soul were buried.

But Betty, poor good woman! she,
You plainly in her face may read it,
Could lend out of that moment's store

THE IDIOT BOY

Five years of happiness or more,
To any that might need it.

But yet I guess that now and then
With Betty all was not so well,
And to the road she turns her ears,
And thence full many a sound she hears, 150
Which she to Susan will not tell.

Poor Susan moans, poor Susan groans,
'As sure as there's a moon in heaven,'
Cries Betty, 'he'll be back again;
'They'll both be here, 'tis almost ten,
'They'll both be here before eleven.'

Poor Susan moans, poor Susan groans,
The clock gives warning for eleven;
'Tis on the stroke—'If Johnny's near,'
Quoth Betty 'he will soon be here, 160
'As sure as there's a moon in heaven.'

The clock is on the stroke of twelve,
And Johnny is not yet in sight,
The moon's in heaven, as Betty sees,
But Betty is not quite at ease;
And Susan has a dreadful night.

And Betty, half an hour ago,
On Johnny vile reflections cast;
'A little idle sauntering thing!'
With other names, an endless string, 170
But now that time is gone and past.

THE IDIOT BOY

And Betty's drooping at the heart,
That happy time all past and gone,
'How can it be he is so late?
'The doctor he has made him wait,
'Susan! they'll both be here anon.'

And Susan's growing worse and worse,
And Betty's in a sad quandary;
And then there's nobody to say
If she must go or she must stay: 180
—She's in a sad quandary.

The clock is on the stroke of one;
But neither Doctor nor his guide
Appear along the moonlight road,
There's neither horse nor man abroad,
And Betty's still at Susan's side.

And Susan she begins to fear
Of sad mischances not a few,
That Johnny may perhaps be drown'd,
Or lost perhaps, and never found;   190
Which they must both for ever rue.

She prefaced half a hint of this
With, 'God forbid it should be true!'
At the first word that Susan said
Cried Betty, rising from the bed,
'Susan, I'd gladly stay with you.

'I must be gone, I must away,
'Consider, Johnny's but half-wise;
'Susan, we must take care of him,

THE IDIOT BOY

'If he is hurt in life or limb'—
'Oh God forbid!' poor Susan cries.

'What can I do?' says Betty, going,
'What can I do to ease your pain?
'Good Susan tell me, and I'll stay;
'I fear you're in a dreadful way,
'But I shall soon be back again.'

'Good Betty go, good Betty go,
'There's nothing that can ease my pain.'
Then off she hies, but with a prayer
That God poor Susan's life would spare,
Till she comes back again.

So, through the moonlight lane she goes,
And far into the moonlight dale;
And how she ran, and how she walked,
And all that to herself she talked,
Would surely be a tedious tale.

In high and low, above, below,
In great and small, in round and square,
In tree and tower was Johnny seen,
In bush and brake, in black and green,
'Twas Johnny, Johnny, every where.

She's past the bridge that's in the dale,
And now the thought torments her sore,
Johnny perhaps his horse forsook,
To hunt the moon that's in the brook,
And never will be heard of more.

THE IDIOT BOY

And now she's high upon the down,
Alone amid a prospect wide;
There's neither Johnny nor his horse,
Among the fern or in the gorse;
There's neither doctor nor his guide.

'Oh saints! what is become of him?
'Perhaps he's climbed into an oak,
'Where he will stay till he is dead;
'Or sadly he has been misled,
'And joined the wandering gypsey-folk.

'Or him that wicked pony's carried
'To the dark cave, the goblins' hall,
'Or in the castle he's pursuing,
'Among the ghosts, his own undoing;
'Or playing with the waterfall.'

At poor old Susan then she railed,
While to the town she posts away;
'If Susan had not been so ill,
'Alas! I should have had him still,
'My Johnny, till my dying day.'

Poor Betty! in this sad distemper,
The doctor's self would hardly spare,
Unworthy things she talked and wild,
Even he, of cattle the most mild,
The pony had his share.

And now she's got into the town,
And to the doctor's door she hies;
'Tis silence all on every side;

The town so long, the town so wide,
Is silent as the skies.

And now she's at the doctor's door,
She lifts the knocker, rap, rap, rap,
The doctor at the casement shews,
His glimmering eyes that peep and doze; 260
And one hand rubs his old night-cap.

'Oh Doctor! Doctor! where's my Johnny?'
'I'm here, what is't you want with me?'
'Oh Sir! you know I'm Betty Foy,
'And I have lost my poor dear boy,
'You know him—him you often see;

'He's not so wise as some folks be,'
'The devil take his wisdom!' said
The Doctor, looking somewhat grim,
'What, woman! should I know of him?' 270
And, grumbling, he went back to bed.

'O woe is me! O woe is me!
'Here will I die; here will I die;
'I thought to find my Johnny here,
'But he is neither far nor near,
'Oh! what a wretched mother I!'

She stops, she stands, she looks about,
Which way to turn she cannot tell.
Poor Betty! it would ease her pain
If she had heart to knock again; 280
—The clock strikes three—a dismal knell!

THE IDIOT BOY

Then up along the town she hies,
No wonder if her senses fail,
This piteous news so much it shock'd her,
She quite forgot to send the Doctor,
To comfort poor old Susan Gale.

And now she's high upon the down,
And she can see a mile of road,
'Oh cruel! I'm almost three-score;
'Such night as this was ne'er before, 290
'There's not a single soul abroad.'

She listens, but she cannot hear
The foot of horse, the voice of man;
The streams with softest sound are flowing,
The grass you almost hear it growing,
You hear it now if e'er you can.

The owlets through the long blue night
Are shouting to each other still:
Fond lovers, yet not quite hob nob,
They lengthen out the tremulous sob. 300
That echoes far from hill to hill.

Poor Betty now has lost all hope,
Her thoughts are bent on deadly sin;
A green-grown pond she just has pass'd,
And from the brink she hurries fast,
Lest she should drown herself therein.

And now she sits her down and weeps;
Such tears she never shed before;
'Oh dear, dear pony! my sweet joy!

THE IDIOT BOY

'Oh carry back my idiot boy!
'And we will ne'er o'erload thee more.'

A thought is come into her head;
'The pony he is mild and good,
'And we have always used him well;
'Perhaps he's gone along the dell,
'And carried Johnny to the wood.'

Then up she springs as if on wings;
She thinks no more of deadly sin;
If Betty fifty ponds should see,
The last of all her thoughts would be,
To drown herself therein.

Oh reader! now that I might tell
What Johnny and his horse are doing!
What they've been doing all this time,
Oh could I put it into rhyme,
A most delightful tale pursuing!

Perhaps, and no unlikely thought!
He with his pony now doth roam
The cliffs and peaks so high that are,
To lay his hands upon a star,
And in his pocket bring it home.

Perhaps he's turned himself about,
His face unto his horse's tail,
And still and mute, in wonder lost,
All like a silent horseman-ghost,
He travels on along the vale.

THE IDIOT BOY

And now, perhaps, he's hunting sheep,
A fierce and dreadful hunter he!
Yon valley, that's so trim and green,
In five months' time, should he be seen,   340
A desart wilderness will be.

Perhaps, with head and heels on fire,
And like the very soul of evil,
He's galloping away, away,
And so he'll gallop on for aye,
The bane of all that dread the devil.

I to the muses have been bound,
These fourteen years, by strong indentures;
Oh gentle muses! let me tell
But half of what to him befel,   350
For sure he met with strange adventures.

Oh gentle muses! is this kind?
Why will ye thus my suit repel?
Why of your further aid bereave me?
And can ye thus unfriended leave me?
Ye muses! whom I love so well.

Who's yon, that, near the waterfall,
Which thunders down with headlong force,
Beneath the moon, yet shining fair,
As careless as if nothing were,   360
Sits upright on a feeding horse?

Unto his horse, that's feeding free,
He seems, I think, the rein to give;
Of moon or stars he takes no heed;

THE IDIOT BOY

Of such we in romances read,
—'Tis Johnny! Johnny! as I live.

And that's the very pony too.
Where is she, where is Betty Foy?
She hardly can sustain her fears;
The roaring water-fall she hears, 370
And cannot find her idiot boy.

Your pony's worth his weight in gold,
Then calm your terrors, Betty Foy!
She's coming from among the trees,
And now, all full in view, she sees
Him whom she loves, her idiot boy.

And Betty sees the pony too:
Why stand you thus Good Betty Foy?
It is no goblin, 'tis no ghost,
'Tis he whom you so long have lost, 380
He whom you love, your idiot boy.

She looks again—her arms are up—
She screams—she cannot move for joy;
She darts as with a torrent's force,
She almost has o'erturned the horse,
And fast she holds her idiot boy.

And Johnny burrs and laughs aloud,
Whether in cunning or in joy,
I cannot tell; but while he laughs,
Betty a drunken pleasure quaffs, 390
To hear again her idiot boy.

And now she's at the pony's tail,
And now she's at the pony's head,
On that side now, and now on this,
And almost stifled with her bliss,
A few sad tears does Betty shed.

She kisses o'er and o'er again,
Him whom she loves, her idiot boy,
She's happy here, she's happy there,
She is uneasy every where;   400
Her limbs are all alive with joy.

She pats the pony, where or when
She knows not, happy Betty Foy!
The little pony glad may be,
But he is milder far than she,
You hardly can perceive his joy.

'Oh! Johnny, never mind the Doctor;
'You've done your best, and that is all.'
She took the reins, when this was said,
And gently turned the pony's head   410
From the loud water-fall.

By this the stars were almost gone,
The moon was setting on the hill,
So pale you scarcely looked at her:
The little birds began to stir,
Though yet their tongues were still.

The pony, Betty, and her boy,
Wind slowly through the woody dale:

THE IDIOT BOY

And who is she, be-times abroad,
That hobbles up the steep rough road? 420
Who is it, but old Susan Gale?

Long Susan lay deep lost in thought,
And many dreadful fears beset her,
Both for her messenger and nurse;
And as her mind grew worse and worse,
Her body it grew better.

She turned, she toss'd herself in bed,
On all sides doubts and terrors met her;
Point after point did she discuss;
And while her mind was fighting thus, 430
Her body still grew better.

'Alas! what is become of them?
'These fears can never be endured,
'I'll to the wood.'—The word scarce said,
Did Susan rise up from her bed,
As if by magic cured.

Away she posts up hill and down,
And to the wood at length is come,
She spies her friends, she shouts a greeting;
Oh me! it is a merry meeting, 440
As ever was in Christendom.

The owls have hardly sung their last,
While our four travellers homeward wend;
The owls have hooted all night long,
And with the owls began my song,
And with the owls must end.

THE IDIOT BOY

For while they all were travelling home,
Cried Betty, 'Tell us Johnny, do,
'Where all this long night you have been,
'What you have heard, what you have seen,   450
'And Johnny, mind you tell us true.'

Now Johnny all night long had heard
The owls in tuneful concert strive;
No doubt too he the moon had seen;
For in the moonlight he had been
From eight o'clock till five.

And thus to Betty's question, he
Made answer, like a traveller bold,
(His very words I give to you,)
'The cocks did crow to-whoo, to-whoo,   460
'And the sun did shine so cold.'
—Thus answered Johnny in his glory,
And that was all his travel's story.

Lines written near Richmond, upon the Thames, at Evening

How rich the wave, in front, imprest
With evening-twilight's summer hues,
While, facing thus the crimson west,
The boat her silent path pursues!
And see how dark the backward stream!
A little moment past, so smiling!
And still, perhaps, with faithless gleam,
Some other loiterer beguiling.

Such views the youthful bard allure,
But, heedless of the following gloom,   10
He deems their colours shall endure
'Till peace go with him to the tomb.
—And let him nurse his fond deceit,
And what if he must die in sorrow!
Who would not cherish dreams so sweet,
Though grief and pain may come to-morrow?

Glide gently, thus for ever glide,
O Thames! that other bards may see,
As lovely visions by thy side
As now, fair river! come to me.   20
Oh glide, fair stream! for ever so;
Thy quiet soul on all bestowing,
'Till all our minds for ever flow,
As thy deep waters now are flowing.

Vain thought! yet be as now thou art,
That in thy waters may be seen
The image of a poet's heart,
How bright, how solemn, how serene!
Such heart did once the poet bless,
Who, pouring here a* *later* ditty,   30
Could find no refuge from distress,
But in the milder grief of pity.

Remembrance! as we glide along,
For him suspend the dashing oar,
And pray that never child of Song

---

* Collins's Ode on the death of Thomson, the last written, I believe, of the poems which were published during his lifetime. This Ode is also alluded to in the next stanza.

May know his freezing sorrows more.
How calm! how still! the only sound,
The dripping of the oar suspended!
—The evening darkness gathers round
By virtue's holiest powers attended.   40

Expostulation and Reply

'Why William, on that old grey stone,
'Thus for the length of half a day,
'Why William, sit you thus alone,
'And dream your time away?

'Where are your books? that light bequeath'd
'To beings else forlorn and blind!
'Up! Up! and drink the spirit breath'd
'From dead men to their kind.

'You look round on your mother earth,
'As if she for no purpose bore you;   10
'As if you were her first-born birth,
'And none had lived before you!'

One morning thus, by Esthwaite lake,
When life was sweet I knew not why,
To me my good friend Matthew spake,
And thus I made reply.

'The eye it cannot chuse but see,
'We cannot bid the ear be still;
'Our bodies feel, where'er they be,
'Against, or with our will.   20

'Nor less I deem that there are powers,
'Which of themselves our minds impress,
'That we can feed this mind of ours,
'In a wise passiveness.

'Think you, mid all this mighty sum
'Of things for ever speaking,
'That nothing of itself will come,
'But we must still be seeking?

'—Then ask not wherefore, here, alone,
'Conversing as I may,   30
'I sit upon this old grey stone,
'And dream my time away.'

The Tables Turned

AN EVENING SCENE, ON THE SAME SUBJECT

Up! up! my friend, and clear your looks,
Why all this toil and trouble?
Up! up! my friend, and quit your books,
Or surely you'll grow double.

The sun above the mountain's head,
A freshening lustre mellow,
Through all the long green fields has spread,
His first sweet evening yellow.

Books! 'tis a dull and endless strife,
Come, hear the woodland linnet,   10
How sweet his music; on my life
There's more of wisdom in it.

And hark! how blithe the throstle sings!
And he is no mean preacher;
Come forth into the light of things,
Let Nature be your teacher.

She has a world of ready wealth,
Our minds and hearts to bless—
Spontaneous wisdom breathed by health,
Truth breathed by chearfulness.

One impulse from a vernal wood
May teach you more of man;
Of moral evil and of good,
Than all the sages can.

Sweet is the lore which nature brings;
Our meddling intellect
Mis-shapes the beauteous forms of things;
—We murder to dissect.

Enough of science and of art;
Close up these barren leaves;
Come forth, and bring with you a heart
That watches and receives.

Old Man Travelling

ANIMAL TRANQUILLITY AND DECAY,
A SKETCH

      The little hedge-row birds,
That peck along the road, regard him not.
He travels on, and in his face, his step,

His gait, is one expression; every limb,
His look and bending figure, all bespeak
A man who does not move with pain, but moves
With thought—He is insensibly subdued
To settled quiet: he is one by whom
All effort seems forgotten, one to whom
Long patience has such mild composure given, 10
That patience now doth seem a thing, of which
He hath no need. He is by nature led
To peace so perfect, that the young behold
With envy, what the old man hardly feels.
—I asked him whither he was bound, and what
The object of his journey; he replied
'Sir! I am going many miles to take
'A last leave of my son, a mariner,
'Who from a sea-fight has been brought to Falmouth,
'And there is dying in an hospital.' 20

The Complaint of a Forsaken Indian Woman

[*When a Northern Indian, from sickness, is unable to continue his journey with his companions; he is left behind, covered over with Deer-skins, and is supplied with water, food, and fuel if the situation of the place will afford it. He is informed of the track which his companions intend to pursue, and if he is unable to follow, or overtake them, he perishes alone in the Desart; unless he should have the good fortune to fall in with some other Tribes of Indians. It is unnecessary to add that the females are equally, or still more, exposed to the same fate. See that very interesting* 10 *work,* Hearne's Journey *from* Hudson's Bay *to the* Northern Ocean. *When the Northern Lights, as the same writer informs us, vary their position in the air, they make a rustling and a crackling noise. This circumstance is alluded to in the first stanza of the following poem.*]

The Complaint, &c.

Before I see another day,
Oh let my body die away!
In sleep I heard the northern gleams;
The stars they were among my dreams;
In sleep did I behold the skies,
I saw the crackling flashes drive;
And yet they are upon my eyes,
And yet I am alive.
Before I see another day,
Oh let my body die away!   10

My fire is dead: it knew no pain;
Yet is it dead, and I remain.
All stiff with ice the ashes lie;
And they are dead, and I will die.
When I was well, I wished to live,
For clothes, for warmth, for food, and fire;
But they to me no joy can give,
No pleasure now, and no desire.
Then here contented will I lie;
Alone I cannot fear to die.   20

Alas! you might have dragged me on
Another day, a single one!

Too soon despair o'er me prevailed;
Too soon my heartless spirit failed;
When you were gone my limbs were stronger,
And Oh how grievously I rue,
That, afterwards, a little longer,
My friends, I did not follow you!
For strong and without pain I lay,
My friends, when you were gone away. 30

My child! they gave thee to another,
A woman who was not thy mother.
When from my arms my babe they took,
On me how strangely did he look!
Through his whole body something ran,
A most strange something did I see;
—As if he strove to be a man,
That he might pull the sledge for me.
And then he stretched his arms, how wild!
Oh mercy! like a little child. 40

My little joy! my little pride!
In two days more I must have died.
Then do not weep and grieve for me;
I feel I must have died with thee.
Oh wind that o'er my head art flying,
The way my friends their course did bend,
I should not feel the pain of dying,
Could I with thee a message send.
Too soon, my friends, you went away;
For I had many things to say. 50

I'll follow you across the snow,
You travel heavily and slow:

THE COMPLAINT

In spite of all my weary pain,
I'll look upon your tents again.
My fire is dead, and snowy white
The water which beside it stood;
The wolf has come to me to-night,
And he has stolen away my food.
For ever left alone am I,
Then wherefore should I fear to die? 60

My journey will be shortly run,
I shall not see another sun,
I cannot lift my limbs to know
If they have any life or no.
My poor forsaken child! if I
For once could have thee close to me,
With happy heart I then would die,
And my last thoughts would happy be.
I feel my body die away,
I shall not see another day. 70

The Convict

The glory of evening was spread through the west;
 —On the slope of a mountain I stood,
While the joy that precedes the calm season of rest
 Rang loud through the meadow and wood.

'And must we then part from a dwelling so fair?'
 In the pain of my spirit I said,
And with a deep sadness I turned, to repair
 To the cell where the convict is laid.

The thick-ribbed walls that o'ershadow the gate
   Resound; and the dungeons unfold:
I pause; and at length, through the glimmering grate,
   That outcast of pity behold.

His black matted head on his shoulder is bent,
   And deep is the sigh of his breath,
And with stedfast dejection his eyes are intent
   On the fetters that link him to death.

'Tis sorrow enough on that visage to gaze,
   That body dismiss'd from his care;
Yet my fancy has pierced to his heart, and pourtrays
   More terrible images there.

His bones are consumed, and his life-blood is dried,
   With wishes the past to undo;
And his crime, through the pains that o'erwhelm him, descried,
   Still blackens and grows on his view.

When from the dark synod, or blood-reeking field,
   To his chamber the monarch is led,
All soothers of sense their soft virtue shall yield,
   And quietness pillow his head.

But if grief, self-consumed, in oblivion would doze,
   And conscience her tortures appease,
'Mid tumult and uproar this man must repose;
   In the comfortless vault of disease.

When his fetters at night have so press'd on his limbs,
   That the weight can no longer be borne,

If, while a half-slumber his memory bedims,
  The wretch on his pallet should turn,

While the jail-mastiff howls at the dull clanking chain,
  From the roots of his hair there shall start
A thousand sharp punctures of cold-sweating pain,
  And terror shall leap at his heart.   40

But now he half-raises his deep-sunken eye,
  And the motion unsettles a tear;
The silence of sorrow it seems to supply,
  And asks of me why I am here.

'Poor victim! no idle intruder has stood
  'With o'erweening complacence our state to compare,
'But one, whose first wish is the wish to be good,
  'Is come as a brother thy sorrows to share.

'At thy name though compassion her nature resign,
  'Though in virtue's proud mouth thy report be a stain,   50
'My care, if the arm of the mighty were mine,
  'Would plant thee where yet thou might'st blossom again.'

Lines written a few miles above Tintern Abbey

ON REVISITING THE BANKS OF THE WYE DURING A TOUR, July 13, 1798

  Five years have passed; five summers, with the length
  Of five long winters! and again I hear
  These waters, rolling from their mountain-springs

With a sweet inland murmur.*—Once again
Do I behold these steep and lofty cliffs,
Which on a wild secluded scene impress
Thoughts of more deep seclusion; and connect
The landscape with the quiet of the sky.
The day is come when I again repose
Here, under this dark sycamore, and view
These plots of cottage-ground, these orchard-tufts,
Which, at this season, with their unripe fruits,
Among the woods and copses lose themselves,
Nor, with their green and simple hue, disturb
The wild green landscape. Once again I see
These hedge-rows, hardly hedge-rows, little lines
Of sportive wood run wild; these pastoral farms
Green to the very door; and wreathes of smoke
Sent up, in silence, from among the trees,
With some uncertain notice, as might seem,
Of vagrant dwellers in the houseless woods,
Or of some hermit's cave, where by his fire
The hermit sits alone.

                    Though absent long,
These forms of beauty have not been to me,
As is a landscape to a blind man's eye:
But oft, in lonely rooms, and mid the din
Of towns and cities, I have owed to them,
In hours of weariness, sensations sweet,
Felt in the blood, and felt along the heart,
And passing even into my purer mind
With tranquil restoration:—feelings too
Of unremembered pleasure; such, perhaps,
As may have had no trivial influence

---

* The river is not affected by the tides a few miles above Tintern.

TINTERN ABBEY

On that best portion of a good man's life;
His little, nameless, unremembered acts
Of kindness and of love. Nor less, I trust,
To them I may have owed another gift,
Of aspect more sublime; that blessed mood,
In which the burthen of the mystery,
In which the heavy and the weary weight 40
Of all this unintelligible world
Is lighten'd:—that serene and blessed mood,
In which the affections gently lead us on,
Until, the breath of this corporeal frame,
And even the motion of our human blood
Almost suspended, we are laid asleep
In body, and become a living soul:
While with an eye made quiet by the power
Of harmony, and the deep power of joy,
We see into the life of things.

                          If this 50
Be but a vain belief, yet, oh! how oft,
In darkness, and amid the many shapes
Of joyless day-light; when the fretful stir
Unprofitable, and the fever of the world,
Have hung upon the beatings of my heart,
How oft, in spirit, have I turned to thee
O sylvan Wye! Thou wanderer through the woods,
How often has my spirit turned to thee!

And now, with gleams of half-extinguish'd thought,
With many recognitions dim and faint, 60
And somewhat of a sad perplexity,
The picture of the mind revives again:
While here I stand, not only with the sense

Of present pleasure, but with pleasing thoughts
That in this moment there is life and food
For future years. And so I dare to hope
Though changed, no doubt, from what I was, when first
I came among these hills; when like a roe
I bounded o'er the mountains, by the sides
Of the deep rivers, and the lonely streams, 70
Wherever nature led; more like a man
Flying from something that he dreads, than one
Who sought the thing he loved. For nature then
(The coarser pleasures of my boyish days,
And their glad animal movements all gone by,)
To me was all in all.—I cannot paint
What then I was. The sounding cataract
Haunted me like a passion: the tall rock,
The mountain, and the deep and gloomy wood,
Their colours and their forms, were then to me 80
An appetite: a feeling and a love,
That had no need of a remoter charm,
By thought supplied, or any interest
Unborrowed from the eye.—That time is past,
And all its aching joys are now no more,
And all its dizzy raptures. Not for this
Faint I, nor mourn nor murmur: other gifts
Have followed, for such loss, I would believe,
Abundant recompence. For I have learned
To look on nature, not as in the hour 90
Of thoughtless youth, but hearing oftentimes
The still, sad music of humanity,
Not harsh nor grating, though of ample power
To chasten and subdue. And I have felt
A presence that disturbs me with the joy
Of elevated thoughts; a sense sublime

Of something far more deeply interfused,
Whose dwelling is the light of setting suns,
And the round ocean, and the living air,
And the blue sky, and in the mind of man, 100
A motion and a spirit, that impels
All thinking things, all objects of all thought,
And rolls through all things. Therefore am I still
A lover of the meadows and the woods,
And mountains; and of all that we behold
From this green earth; of all the mighty world
Of eye and ear, both what they half-create,*
And what perceive; well pleased to recognize
In nature and the language of the sense,
The anchor of my purest thoughts, the nurse, 110
The guide, the guardian of my heart, and soul
Of all my moral being.

              Nor, perchance,
If I were not thus taught, should I the more
Suffer my genial spirits to decay:
For thou art with me, here, upon the banks
Of this fair river; thou, my dearest Friend,
My dear, dear Friend, and in thy voice I catch
The language of my former heart, and read
My former pleasures in the shooting lights
Of thy wild eyes. Oh! yet a little while 120
May I behold in thee what I was once,
My dear, dear Sister! And this prayer I make,
Knowing that Nature never did betray
The heart that loved her; 'tis her privilege,

---

* This line has a close resemblance to an admirable line of Young, the exact expression of which I cannot recollect.

Through all the years of this our life, to lead
From joy to joy: for she can so inform
The mind that is within us, so impress
With quietness and beauty, and so feed
With lofty thoughts, that neither evil tongues,
Rash judgments, nor the sneers of selfish men, 130
Nor greetings where no kindness is, nor all
The dreary intercourse of daily life,
Shall e'er prevail against us, or disturb
Our chearful faith that all which we behold
Is full of blessings. Therefore let the moon
Shine on thee in thy solitary walk;
And let the misty mountain winds be free
To blow against thee: and in after years,
When these wild ecstasies shall be matured
Into a sober pleasure, when thy mind 140
Shall be a mansion for all lovely forms,
Thy memory be as a dwelling-place
For all sweet sounds and harmonies; Oh! then,
If solitude, or fear, or pain, or grief,
Should be thy portion, with what healing thoughts
Of tender joy wilt thou remember me,
And these my exhortations! Nor, perchance,
If I should be, where I no more can hear
Thy voice, nor catch from thy wild eyes these gleams
Of past existence, wilt thou then forget 150
That on the banks of this delightful stream
We stood together; and that I, so long
A worshipper of Nature, hither came,
Unwearied in that service: rather say
With warmer love, oh! with far deeper zeal
Of holier love. Nor wilt thou then forget,
That after many wanderings, many years

TINTERN ABBEY

Of absence, these steep woods and lofty cliffs,
And this green pastoral landscape, were to me
More dear, both for themselves, and for thy sake. 160

END

ERRATA[1]

[1] [*Corrected in this reprint.*]

Page
- 10 for 'fog smoke-white,' read 'fog-smoke white.'
- 14   'those,' read 'these.'
- 31   Omit the comma after 'loveth well.'
- 80   after 'clanking hour,' place a comma.
- 112 omit the fifteenth line from the bottom,
      'And the low copses coming from the trees.'

COMMENTARY

P. 3. The Advertisement to *Lyrical Ballads*, 1798, was presumably written by Wordsworth, since it is concerned mainly with his poems and theories, and since most of its ideas reappear in his Prefaces of 1800 and 1802.

§ 1. It is . . . human mind] Cf. Preface (1802), pp. 166–7 ('The Poet writes . . . as a Man'), 167 ('To this knowledge . . . attention'), and 169 ('But these passions . . . passions of men').

§ 2. They were written . . . pleasure] A modified account appears in the early paragraphs of the Preface.

Readers . . . title] Repeated in essentials in Preface (1802), p. 155, fn. 9.

It is desirable . . . decision] Restated in Preface (p. 177: 'I have one request', &c.).

§ 3. elder writers] Writers of ballads (cf. 'the elder poets', § 5, below)? Or Shakespeare and Milton (cf. Preface, p. 160)?

those in modern times] Probably Burns and Cowper, who are often mentioned in this sense at this time by Wordsworth and Coleridge.

manners] 'The modes of life, customary rules of behaviour, conditions of society, prevailing in a people' (*O.E.D.*, sense 4. c).

§ 4. An accurate taste . . . composition] Repeated in Preface, p. 177. Observations of this kind are scattered throughout the *Discourses* of Reynolds: see, for instance, Discourse XII (1784): 'The habit of contemplating and brooding over the ideas of great geniuses, till you find yourself warmed by the contact, is the true method of forming an artist-like mind . . . the taste [is formed] by such an intercourse'.

§ 5. Goody Blake . . . the Thorn . . . Expostulation and Reply] See the Preface, p. 174, and the notes to the poems.

three last centuries] Why from 1498? Perhaps Wordsworth means 'from Chaucer's day' (cf. Preface, p. 157, Wordsworth's fn.) and miscalculates by a century.

P. 7. *The Rime of the Ancyent Marinere*. By Coleridge. Written November 1797–March 1798: see *E.Y.*, p. 194 (20 November 1797, the earliest mention of the poem): 'William [Wordsworth] and

COMMENTARY 119

Coleridge employing themselves in laying the plan of a ballad, to be published with some pieces of William's'; *Journals*, i. 13 (23 March 1798): 'Coleridge ... brought his ballad finished'. On 6 January 1798 Coleridge proposed to 'sell my Ballad' to the *Monthly Magazine* for £5 (*C.L.*, i. 368), but he did not. On 18 February he had 'finished my ballad—it is 340 lines' (658 lines in the text of *L.B.*; *C.L.*, i. 387 and n.).

The numerous revisions of the poem can be traced in *C.P.W.*, i. 186–209; some of the more notable are given below. Many designed to remove archaisms and other quaintnesses were made in the edition of 1800; see the list of emendations in *C.L.*, i. 598–602 (Coleridge to Biggs and Cottle, mid-July 1800).

For further information on the genesis of the poem, see the I.F. note to *We are Seven*, printed below, p. 135. The passage from Shelvocke to which Wordsworth refers there is given below, note to 61–80. Coleridge's 'friend Mr. Cruickshank' is John Cruikshank, brother of the 'most gentle maid' of Coleridge's *The Nightingale*, 69, of whose dream we know no more than that it involved the skeleton ship (see note to 169–72, below).

The most famous study of this, Coleridge's most famous poem, is John Livingston Lowes, *The Road to Xanadu* (London, 1927), an exhaustive survey of the many literary sources which went to the making of the poem, and of the means by which they were combined. It is impossible to summarize the findings of this book here, but I have tried to indicate the more important of Coleridge's debts to the seventeenth- and eighteenth-century books of travel which supplied much of his imagery and diction, especially in the early part of the poem. Rather than burden the notes with long quotations from, and long titles of, not very accessible books, I have simply indicated that such and such a phrase or image is from 'the voyagers' and given a reference to Lowes's discussion.

Since the text of 1798 printed here is the version most extreme in its archaisms and other oddities of language and style, I have given brief indications of Coleridge's sources in this field also. The notes concerned are often based on Lowes, Chapter XVII.

A useful anthology of criticism of the poem, contemporary and modern, may be found in *The Rime of the Ancient Mariner: A Handbook*, ed. Royal A. Gettmann (San Francisco, 1961).

5, 7. Lowes (p. 546) notes a possible borrowing from William Taylor's translation of Bürger's *Lenore*: 'The wedding guests thy coming waite, The chamber dore is ope'. The translation (published 1796) caused a considerable stir in literary circles at the time. Lowes (p. 251) traces the association of the mysterious and compelling Mariner with the wedding feast to Schiller's *Der Geisterseher*, the source of the plot of Coleridge's play *Osorio*, on which he had been working (March–October 1797) just before he began planning *A.M.* Coleridge in 1795–6 proposed the Wandering Jew as the subject of 'a romance' (*C.N.B.*, i. 45), and is reported to have envisaged the Mariner as 'the everlasting wandering Jew—had told this story ten thousand times since the voyage, which was in his early youth and 50 years before' (*C.N.B.*, i. 45, note).

19–20. Wordsworth claims to have written these lines: see the I.F. note to *We are Seven*, p. 136 below.

29, 81. This method of indicating direction of travel Coleridge probably took from a passage of Herodotus: 'Thus two years having elapsed, they [the Phoenicians] returned to Egypt, passing by the Pillars of Hercules; and they reported a circumstance which I can scarcely credit, but other people may, *that sailing round Lybia the sun rose on the right hand*' (Lowes, p. 127).

39–40. Cf. Chaucer, *Cant. Tales*, F. 268: 'Toforn hym gooth the loude mynstralcye'.

49–52. Mist and Snow . . . wond'rous cauld . . . Ice mast-high . . . As green as Emerauld] Phrases from the voyagers (Lowes, pp. 140–1). The form 'cauld' is common in traditional ballads; cf. 'Auld', *Goody Blake*, 21.

53. *Drifts* 'floating ice' and *clifts* 'clefts, fissures' are both voyagers' words (Lowes, pp. 143–5).

55. Ne] Chaucerian or Spenserian negative, used frequently in this version and removed in *L.B.*, 1800.

59. The verbs are from the voyagers (Lowes, p. 146); *swound* 'swoon' (60) is from an account of incipient suffocation among voyagers trying to warm themselves on the ice (Lowes, p. 147).

COMMENTARY

61-80. The central incident of the albatross and its shooting was suggested by Wordsworth on the basis of an anecdote in Shelvocke's *Voyage Round the World* . . . (London, 1726), pp. 72-73: 'We had continual squals of sleet, snow and rain, and the heavens were perpetually hid from us by gloomy dismal clouds. In short, one would think it impossible that any thing living could subsist in so rigid a climate; and, indeed, we all observed, that we had not had the sight of one fish of any kind, since we were come to the Southward of the streights of *le Mair*, nor one sea-bird, except a disconsolate black *Albitross*, who accompanied us for several days, hovering about us as if he had lost himself, till *Hatley*, (my second Captain) observing, in one of his melancholy fits, that this bird was always hovering near us, imagin'd, from his colour, that it might be some ill omen. That which, I suppose, induced him the more to encourage his superstition, was the continued series of contrary tempestuous winds, which had oppress'd us ever since we had got into this sea. But be that as it would, he, after some fruitless attempts, at length, shot the *Albitross*, not doubting (perhaps) that we should have a fair wind after it' (Lowes, p. 226). In 1804 Coleridge records seeing a hawk similarly shot at during his voyage to Malta, and comments: 'Poor Hawk! O Strange Lust of Murder in Man!—It is not cruelty / it is mere non-feeling from non-thinking' (*C.N.B.*, ii. 2090).

63. an] Used to mean 'as if', rather than 'if'; cf. 147. Both occurrences were altered to 'as if' in 1800.

65. From an account of Magellan's voyage (Lowes, p. 150): 'having . . . consumed all their Bisket and other Victuals, they fell into such necessitie, that they were inforced to eate the powder that remayned thereof; being now full of Wormes'. This detail was removed in 1800.

67. split . . . Thunder] From the voyagers (Lowes, pp. 146-7).

69-72. good south wind . . . Marinere's hollo] From the voyagers (Lowes, pp. 148-9).

75. fog-smoke white] From the voyagers (Lowes, pp. 148-9).

83. weft] Nautical term for a signal-flag: see Lowes, pp. 261 ff. Removed in 1800.

93-94. From the voyagers (Lowes, pp. 155-7), or Robert South,

122   COMMENTARY

Sermons (1737), v. 165: 'Christ, the great Sun of Righteousness, & Saviour of the World, having by a glorious rising after a red & bloody setting, proclaimed his Deity to men & angels', cited in *C.N.B.*, i. 327.

94. uprist] Chaucerian archaism, revived in the eighteenth century.

95–98. The opinion of the crew is that of Captain Hatley who shot the albatross in Shelvocke's *Voyage*; see note on 61–80.

99. breezes] Voyagers' word for the Trade Winds (Lowes, pp. 129–30). Altered in 1817 to the more familiar form 'fair breeze'.

100. Altered to 'The furrow stream'd off free' in 1817, on the basis of Coleridge's observations during his voyage to Malta in 1804; the original reading was restored in 1828. In 1817 Coleridge rejected the original reading by observing that 'this was the image as seen by a spectator from the shore, or from another vessel. From the ship itself, the *Wake* appears like a brook flowing off from the stern' (*C.P. W.*, i. 190). Cf. *C.N.B.*, ii. 1996 and note.

101–2. Similar phrasing used of Magellan's voyage (Lowes, p. 130).

107–8, 110. Phrasing perhaps from Gilbert's White's *Natural History of Selborne* (1789), or from Thomas Burnet's *Telluris Theoria Sacra* (1681–9); see Lowes, pp. 158–60.

109. From the voyagers (Lowes, p. 158).

121–2. From the voyagers (Lowes, pp. 87–89).

127–30. Wordsworth suggested that 'the tutelary Spirits of [the South Sea take upon them to avenge the crime' of shooting the albatross; see I.F. note to *We are Seven*, below, p. 135.

133. Ab out, about] Shakespeare, *Macbeth*, I. iii. 34—a witch-scene, proba bly suggesting 'witch's oils' in 135.

135–6. The colours from a description of phosphorescence by Captain Cook; 'oils' from a description of the sea in *Philosophical Transactions of the Royal Society of London*, v; 'burnt' from the voyagers (Lowes, pp. 81–84).

140. Possibly from the voyagers (Lowes, p. 500).

144. wist] 'was aware of'. A Chaucerian archaism, common in various eighteenth-century poets (Lowes, p. 335).

156. 'I took the thought of "*grinning for joy*" . . . from poor Burnett's remark to me, when we had climbed to the top of Plin-

COMMENTARY 123

limmon, and were nearly dead with thirst. We could not speak for the constriction, till we found a little puddle under a stone. He said to me,—"You grinned like an idiot!" He had done the same' (Coleridge, *Table Talk*, 31 May 1830). He refers to a walking tour in North Wales in Summer 1794; Lowes (p. 210) notes that 'Burnett' should be 'Berdmore' or 'Brookes', and that 'Plinlimmon' should be 'Penmaenmawr' (see *C.L.*, i. 94).

161. Withouten] Archaism from ballads, e.g. *Chevy Chase*, *Battle of Otterbourne*, in Percy's *Reliques*.

161, 163-4. Spectral ships in voyagers' tales sail without (or against) wind or tide at sunset (Lowes, pp. 275-6).

165, 175. western wave . . . Sails that glance in the Sun] Probably from William Gilbert's poem *The Hurricane* (Lowes, p. 202). Lowes (p. 201) also compares 175-6 with *Journals*, i. 7 (8 February 1798): 'Sat a considerable time upon the heath. Its surface restless and glittering with . . . the waving of the spiders' threads'.

169-72, 179-80. According to Wordsworth (as cited by Alexander Dyce), the dream of Coleridge's friend John Cruikshank which gave the first hint of the poem involved 'a skeleton ship, with figures in it' (Lowes, p. 223).

180. Pheere] 'companion'; a ballad word which Coleridge could find in *Sir Cauline*, in Percy's *Reliques*, or in Chatterton.

181, 188, 192. Lowes (p. 277) cites a Dutch folk tale 'of one Falkenberg, who, for murder done, is doomed to wander forever on the sea, accompanied by two spectral forms, one white, one black, [who] play at dice for the wanderer's soul.' He thinks that Coleridge may have heard such a story in Devon or Bristol. Miss Coburn (*C.N.B.*, i. 97, note) finds similar details in the figures of Remorse and Misery in Thomas Sackville's *Induction* to *The Mirror for Magistrates*, from which Coleridge made extracts in 1796. He removed the 'Gothic' details of 181-5 in 1817.

182. ween] Ballad archaism from *Sir Cauline*.

195. sterte] 'started'; archaism from Chaucer or *Sir Cauline*.

199. The more familiar version, 'With far-heard whisper, o'er the sea', appeared in 1817. The revision, along with others about this point, has been attributed to Coleridge's observations on his voyage

to Malta in 1804; see *C.N.B.*, ii. 2086 (10 May 1804): 'a calm / and between 4 & 5 the Ships so near each other that the Cocks answered each other from 2 or 3 Coops', and note. This may be, as Coleridge says, a 'sweet Image for a Calm', but 'far-heard' and 'whisper' do not accord with 'so near' and the cry of cocks. An intermediate version (*C.P.W.*, i. 195; *C.N.B.*, ii. 2880) which adds the image 'The helmsman's face by his lamp gleam'd bright', certainly observed on the Malta voyage (*C.N.B.*, ii. 2001), retains 'With never a whisper'.

200. The text of 1798 prints 'Oft', uncorrected in the Errata but in several copies corrected to 'Off' with a pen.

201. clombe] 'climbed'. Often called an archaism, but the form is used by the Wordsworth family (e.g. *Prel.*, VI. 562) as a normal past tense.

202. The horned Moon] Mentioned in *Journals*, i. 13 (21 and 23 March 1798; the latter entry records also the completion of the poem). The detail of the star is probably from *Philosophical Transactions of the Royal Society*, v (Lowes, p. 41).

207. ee] Archaism from *Sir Cauline*; cf. *een*, 445, 448.

218–19. In a note of 1817 Coleridge attributes these lines to Wordsworth.

234. eldritch] Ballad word in *Sir Cauline*, glossed by Percy as 'wild, hideous, ghostly'. In 1800 altered to 'ghastly'; in 1817 to 'rotting' as in 232.

242. Probably from Vergil, *Aeneid*, III. 193: 'caelum undique et undique pontus', rather than English sources also hinted at by Lowes, p. 566.

260. yspread] Chaucerian archaism, removed in 1800.

262–3. Probably from the voyagers (Lowes, p. 89).

264–73. Phrasing probably from William Falconer's *The Shipwreck* (Lowes, pp. 52–53).

265. water-snakes] From William Dampier's *New Voyage round the World* (Lowes, p. 49).

286. yeven] 'given'; Chaucerian form, altered to 'given' in 1800.

289. silly] The sense is not clear; perhaps 'Plain, simple, rustic, homely' (*O.E.D.*, sense 3. c, quoting this passage).

306. fire-flags] Lowes (p. 189) traces the image to Samuel Hearne's

COMMENTARY 125

account of the Aurora Borealis; see the last sentence quoted in note on *The Complaint of a Forsaken Indian Woman*, p. 148.

309. The visibility of the stars through the Aurora is mentioned in a note to Erasmus Darwin's *Botanic Garden* which Coleridge transcribed (Lowes, pp. 189–90). In later readings of this line he adopted the phrasing of Darwin's verse to which the note refers.

312–18. The phrasing is from William Bartram, *Travels through North and South Carolina* ... (1791) (Lowes, pp. 186–7).

327 ff. Wordsworth (I.F. note to *We are Seven*) claims to have suggested 'the navigation of the ship by the dead men'. Lowes (pp. 281 ff.) notes that in texts of 1800 and later Coleridge explains that the dead bodies are animated by 'a troop of spirits blest', and suggests that Coleridge took this motif and others from an epistle of Paulinus, Bishop of Nola (b. 353).

329. 'gan] Though marked as an abbreviation for 'began', the effect is like the Chaucerian *gan* used more or less as an auxiliary of the past tense.

347–55. Diction ('Lavrock', 'jargoning', 'an angel's song') from the Chaucerian translation of *The Romance of the Rose* (Lowes, pp. 333–4).

373. beforne] Archaism from *Sir Cauline*.

375. n'old] 'would not'; Chaucerian form. This stanza (and the three preceding) were removed in 1800.

451–6. The simile is from Dante, *Inferno*, XXI. 25–30 (Lowes, p. 526).

466. sail'd softly] From the voyagers (Lowes, p. 324).

472. Probably from the voyagers (Lowes, p. 154).

527. Eftsones] Chaucerian archaism, altered to 'But soon' in 1800.

579–84. The description of the moving sound seems to have been suggested by eighteenth-century descriptions of earthquakes in the *Philosophical Transactions of the Royal Society* (Lowes, pp. 289–91).

610. What manner man] Chaucerian archaism, altered to 'What manner of man' in 1817.

645–50. It was presumably this passage that Coleridge had in mind when, in reply to Mrs. Barbauld's criticism that the poem 'had no moral', he said that 'in my own judgment the poem had too much; and that the only, or chief fault, if I might say so, was the obtrusion of the moral sentiment so openly on the reader as a principle or cause of action in a work of such pure imagination. It ought to have had no more moral than the Arabian Nights' tale of the merchant's sitting down to eat dates by the side of a well, and throwing the shells aside, and lo! a genie starts up, and says he *must* kill the aforesaid merchant, *because* one of the date shells had, it seems, put out the eye of the genie's son' (*Table Talk*, 31 May 1830).

P. 32. *The Foster-Mother's Tale*. An extract from Coleridge's play *Osorio* (1797), Act IV; omitted from the text of the revised, acting version of the play, called *Remorse* (London, 1813), but printed as an appendix to the second edition of *Remorse* (also published in 1813). For the original version of the passage, see *C.P.W.*, ii. 571–4.

Albert, the elder son of Velez, is supposed by his father to have been drowned, and by his villainous younger brother, Osorio, to have been murdered at his, Osorio's, instigation. He is, in fact, alive, and returns to the neighbourhood in the guise of a Moorish conjurer. Unrecognized by his beloved, Maria, or by Osorio, he is employed by Osorio to take part in a conjuring performance designed to persuade Maria of his own death. At the end of the performance, Albert instructs Maria to meet him at the cottage of their common foster-mother. He is subsequently arrested by the Inquisition for sorcery, and thrown into Velez's dungeon, where (Act V) he utters the soliloquy printed in *L.B.* as *The Dungeon* (pp. 80–81). Maria visits the foster-mother and hears the tale printed here, which has no relevance to the plot of *Osorio*.

P. 35. *Lines left upon a Seat in a Yew-tree*. I.F.: 'Composed in part at school at Hawkshead. The tree has disappeared, and the slip of common on which it stood, that ran parallel to the lake and lay open to it, has long been enclosed, so that the road has lost much of its attraction. This spot was my favourite walk in the evenings during the latter part of my School-time. The individual whose habits and character are here given was a gentleman of the neighbourhood, a man of talent and learning who had been educated at one of our Universities, and returned to pass his time in seclusion on his own estate. He died a bachelor in middle age. Induced by the beauty of the prospect, he built a small summerhouse on the rocks above the

COMMENTARY 127

peninsula on which the ferry-house stands. This property afterwards past into the hands of the late Mr. Curwen. The site was long ago pointed out by Mr. West in his Guide as the pride of the Lakes, and now goes by the name of "The Station." So much used I to be delighted with the view from it, while a little boy, that some years before the first pleasure-house was built, I led thither from Hawkshead a youngster about my own age, an Irish Boy who was a servant to an Itinerant Conjurer. My motive was to witness the pleasure I expected the boy would receive from the prospect of the islands below and the intermingling water. I was not disappointed; and I hope the fact, insignificant as it may seem to some, may be thought worthy of note by others who may cast their eye over these notes.'

In spite of the dating implied here, the poem, as de Selincourt points out (*W.P.W.*, i. 329), probably originates mainly in 1795, since it represents Wordsworth's 'revulsion from the intellectual arrogance and self-sufficiency of Godwinism'; and it was in a form earlier than that given here in a MS. of 1797.

On the 'individual whose habits and character are here given' and the site, see West's *Guide to the Lakes in Cumberland, Westmorland, and Lancashire* (8th ed., Kendal, 1802), pp. 55–56: 'The road to the ferry [across Windermere] is round the head of Estwaite-water, through the villages of Colthouse and Sawreys. Ascend a steep hill, and from its summit, have a view of a long reach of Windermerewater, stretching far to the south, till lost between two high promontories. The road serpentizes round a rocky mountain, till you come under a broken scar, that in some places hangs over the way, and where ancient yews and hollies grow fantastically amongst the fallen rocks. This brings you soon to

'STATION I. Near the isthmus of the ferry point, observe two small oak trees that inclose the road; these will guide you to this celebrated station . . . The rock rises perpendicularly from the lake, and forms a pretty bay★.

'★In consequence of the act for inclosing Claif-Common, the late Rev. W. Brathwaite purchased the ground including this station, and erected an elegant and commodious building thereon, for the entertainment of his friends, called *Belle-Vieu*; he also planted the adjoining grounds, and altered the direction of the road, which was rugged and unsafe, and rendered it more convenient by carrying it nearer the margin of the lake.—This place has since been purchased by Mr. Curwen.'

An unpublished draft for Wordsworth's *Guide to the Lakes* (Grasmere MS. Prose 23) speaks of 'the remnant of a decaying yew tree' 'yet to be seen', and the 'seat from which the solitary humour of the framer may not unfairly be inferred ... the boughs had been trained to bend round the seat and almost embrace the Person sitting within allowing only an opening for the beautiful landscape' (cf. ll. 10–11 of the poem).

In 1815 classed as a poem of 'Sentiment and Reflection'; in 1845 transferred to 'Poems written in Youth'.

25–26. with juniper ... o'er] Cf. MS. Prose 23: 'The narrow space between the yew tree & the Lake was scattered over with juniper, furze, heath, & wild time [*sic*].'

53–55. A reference may be intended to Matthew, v. 22: 'whosoever shall say, Thou fool, shall be in danger of hellfire.'

P. 37. *The Nightingale*. By Coleridge. The poem was completed by 10 May 1798, when Coleridge sent it to Wordsworth under the cover of a comic verse-letter (*C.L.*, i. 406). See Introd., sec. II. The subject is common in magazine poems; see Introd., sec. IV, n. 2. The poem 'duplicates the inexhaustible and varied flow of [Coleridge's] talk with startling fidelity. The meter underscores each pause and shift of thought' (Max F. Schulz, *The Poetic Voices of Coleridge* [Detroit, 1963], p. 78).

13. 'Most musical, most melancholy'] Milton, *Il Penseroso*, 62.

24–30. Cf. a fragment by Wordsworth in 'a notebook containing the first extant MS. of "Christabel" ' (1798–9), printed in *W.P.W.*, v. 343–4:

> In many a walk
> At evening or by moonlight, or reclined
> At midday upon beds of forest moss,
> Have we to Nature and her impulses
> Of our whole being made free gift ...

COMMENTARY 129

The uncertainty of dating makes it impossible to decide which poet, if either, is borrowing from the other.

39. Philomela] Ovid, *Metamorphoses*, VI. 424 ff. Tereus, king of Thrace, ravished his sister-in-law Philomela, and cut out her tongue to prevent her revealing the deed. She wove the story into a tapestry which she sent to her sister Procne, who in revenge killed her son Itys and served the body as a meal to Tereus. As Tereus pursued the sisters in his rage, he was changed to a hoopoe, Procne to a swallow, and Philomela to a nightingale.

40. My Friend, and my Friend's Sister] William and Dorothy Wordsworth.

50. a castle] Enmore, the home of the Earl of Egmont.

59. skirmish] *O.E.D.*, sense 3. b: 'a slight display of something'?

64–69. On moonlight . . . love-torch.] Omitted after 1798.

65. leafits] To judge from the quotations in *O.E.D.*, probably a technical term from botany. Literary uses quoted are all later than 1798. By March 1801 (and probably earlier) Coleridge was studying William Withering, *An Arrangement of British Plants* (1796); see *C.N.B.*, i. 863, and *E.Y.*, p. 321.

69. A most gentle maid] Ellen Cruikshank. Her father was the agent to the Earl of Egmont, and her brother John the source of the skeleton ship of *The Ancient Mariner* (see note to *A.M.*, 169–72, above).

82. airy harps] Wind-harps, Aeolian harps. Cf. Coleridge's *The Eolian Harp*, 12–25 (*C.P.W.*, i. 100–1).

90. That strain again] Shakespeare, *Twelfth Night*, I. i. 4.

91. Babe] David Hartley Coleridge (1796–1849). Cf. *C.N.B.*, i. 219 (?Autumn 1797): 'Hartley fell down & hurt himself—I caught him up crying & screaming—& ran out of doors with him.—The Moon caught his eye—he ceased crying immediately—& his eyes & the tears in them, how they glittered in the Moonlight!' For the sentiment of 106–9, cf. Coleridge's *Frost at Midnight* (also published in 1798), 44 ff. (*C.P.W.*, i. 242).

107–9. A practical application of the associationist psychology of David Hartley (*Observations on Man*, 1749), whose thinking Coleridge had not yet rejected and after whom he had named his son.

P. 41. *The Female Vagrant*. Part of the longer poem now called *Guilt and Sorrow*, corresponding to ll. 199–450 of the standard text of that work. *Guilt and Sorrow* was begun during the early nineties, but was not published until 1842, in the volume entitled *Poems, Chiefly of Early and Late Years*. The Female Vagrant was reprinted in all editions of *L.B.* after 1798 (1800, 1802, 1805), in Wordsworth's *Poems* of 1815, and in subsequent editions of the collected poems until the appearance of the complete *Guilt and Sorrow* in 1842. The I.F. note to *Guilt and Sorrow* runs: 'Unwilling to be unnecessarily particular, I have assigned this Poem to the dates 93 and 94, but in fact much of the "Female Vagrant's" story was composed at least two years before. All that relates to her sufferings as a Soldier's wife in America and her condition of mind during her voyage home were faithfully taken from the report made to me of her own case by a friend who had been subjected to the same trials and affected in the same way. Mr. Coleridge, when I first became acquainted with him, was so much impressed with this Poem that it would have incouraged me to publish the whole as it then stood; but the Mariner's fate appeared to me so tragical as to require a treatment more subdued and yet more strictly applicable in expression than I had at first given to it. This fault was corrected nearly 50 years afterwards when I determined to publish the whole. It may be worth while to remark that tho' the incidents of this attempt do only in a small degree produce each other and it deviates accordingly from the general rule by which narrative pieces ought to be governed, it is not therefore wanting in continuous hold upon the mind or in unity which is effected by the identity of moral interest[?s] that places the two personages upon the same footing in the reader's sympathies. My ramble over many parts of Salisbury plain put me, as mentioned in the preface, upon writing this Poem, and left on my mind imaginative impressions the force of wh[ich] I have felt to this day. From that district I proceeded to Bath, Bristol, and so on to the banks of the Wye, where I took again to travelling on foot. In remembrance of that part of my journey which was in 93 I began the verses—"Five years have passed &c.—"' The I.F. note to *The Female Vagrant* runs: 'I find that the date of this is placed in 1792 in contradiction, by mistake, to what I

COMMENTARY 131

have asserted in "Guilt and Sorrow." The correct date is 1793-4. The chief incident[s] of it, more particularly the description of her feelings on the Atlantic are taken from life.'

In 1815 the poem was classified under 'Juvenile Pieces'; it remained in this class (later called 'Poems written in Youth') in this form and as *Guilt and Sorrow*.

The thirty stanzas of the present text correspond more or less to stanzas 26-44 of Wordsworth's first surviving MS. of *Guilt and Sorrow*, that entitled *Salisbury Plain* and designated MS. 1 in *W.P.W.*, i. 330 ff. (Grasmere MS. Verse 11). The following stanzas of *The Female Vagrant* are not represented in the MS.: 2, 12, 13, 18, 21-29; *The Female Vagrant*, stanzas 5-6, correspond to stanza 29 of the MS.; and the following stanzas of the MS. are not represented in *The Female Vagrant*: 1-25, 37-39, 45-61. Wordsworth's major revisions to the poem are thus later than our text and need not be pursued here. See *W.P.W.*, i. 331 ff., and the textual notes to *Guilt and Sorrow*, ibid., 106 ff.

The poem is in the Spenserian stanza and retains, in this early version, traces of the poetic diction of eighteenth-century imitators of Spenser such as Thomson in *The Castle of Indolence* (1748); note ★'fleecy store' (8); 'May's dewy prime' (25); ★'snowy pride' (27); 'equinoctial deep' (110); ★the personifications of 157-62; ★'wild brood' (215); 'vagrant ease' (219); ★'milky udder' (225). The starred examples were removed or altered as the poem was revised. No source for the tale has been discovered except the hearsay recorded in the I.F. notes.

117. devoted] 'doomed'.

172. Cf. *King Lear*, IV. vii. 63: 'I fear I am not in my perfect mind'.

P. 50. *Goody Blake and Harry Gill*. I.F.: 'Written at Alfoxden 1798. The incident from Dr. Darwin's Zoonomia.' Mentioned briefly in Advertisement, 1798 (p. 4, above); discussed in Preface, 1800 (p. 174, below). In 1815 classified under 'Poems of the Imagination', on the curious ground that *The Horn of Egremont Castle* and *Goody Blake*, 'as they rather refer to the imagination than are produced by it, would not have been placed here but to avoid a needless multiplication of the Classes' (*Poems*, 1815, i. 316). In 1845 transferred to 'Miscellaneous Poems'; in the same edition the account in the Preface to

132   COMMENTARY

L.B. disappeared. The source, as I.F. indicates, is Erasmus Darwin, *Zoonomia, or the Laws of Organic Life* (London, 1796), ii. 359: 'I received good information of the truth of the following case, which was published a few years ago in the newspapers. A young farmer in Warwickshire, finding his hedges broke, and the sticks carried away during a frosty season, determined to watch for the thief. He lay many cold hours under a hay-stack, and at length an old woman, like a witch in a play, approached, and began to pull up the hedge; he waited till she had tied up her bottle of sticks, and was carrying them off, that he might convict her of the theft, and then springing from his concealment, he seized his prey with violent threats. After some altercation, in which her load was left upon the ground, she kneeled upon her bottle of sticks, and raising her arms to Heaven beneath the bright moon then at the full, spoke to the farmer already shivering with cold, "Heaven grant, that thou never mayest know again the blessing to be warm." He complained of cold all the next day, and wore an upper coat, and in a few days another, and in a fortnight took to his bed, always saying nothing made him warm, he covered himself with very many blankets, and had a sieve over his face, as he lay; and from this one insane idea he kept his bed above twenty years for fear of the cold air, till at length he died.' Darwin cites this as a case of '*Mania mutabilis*. Mutable madness'; 'Where the patients are liable to mistake ideas of sensation for those of irritation, that is, imaginations for realities' (p. 356). Wordsworth borrowed Darwin's book from Joseph Cottle in 1798 (*E.Y.*, p. 199). He may have taken Harry's surname from Joseph Gill, the caretaker of Racedown Lodge, where Wordsworth lived from September 1795 to July 1797.

39. *canty*] Attributed by *O.E.D.* to Scottish and northern English dialect: 'Cheerful, lively, gladsome . . . in north of England rather = lively, brisk, active'.

P. 55. *Lines written at a small distance* . . . Composed 1798. Subsequently called *To my Sister* (1845 and later editions). I.F.: 'Composed in front of Alfoxden House. My little boy messenger on this occasion was the son of Basil Montagu. The larch mentioned in the first stanza was standing when I revisited the place in May 1841, more than 40 years after. [The rest of the note discusses the larch and

COMMENTARY 133

a beech near by.]' In 1815 classified under 'Poems proceeding from Sentiment and Reflection'.

Dorothy Wordsworth records of 3 March 1798, 'A very mild, cloudy evening'; of 6 March, 'a mild, pleasant afternoon'; of 9 March, 'The day very warm' (*Journals*, i. 11–12).

17–20. We shall not feel compelled to begin the year with 1 January as formal calendars do.

29–30. Since this is the first day of the year in 'Our living Calendar' (18), New Year resolutions are appropriate.

33–34. Cf. *Lines written . . . above Tintern Abbey*, 101–3: 'A motion and a spirit, that . . . rolls through all things'.

P. 57. *Simon Lee*. Composed 1798. I.F.: 'This old man had been huntsman to the Squires of Alfoxden, which, at the time we occupied it belonged to a minor. The old man's cottage stood upon the common a little way from the entrance to Alfoxden Park. But it had disappeared. Many other changes had taken place in the adjoining village, which I could not but notice with a regret more natural than well-considered. Improvements but rarely appear such to those who, after long intervals of time, revisit places they have had much pleasure in. It is unnecessary to add, the fact was as mentioned in the poem, and I have, after an interval of 45 years, the image of the old man as fresh before my eyes as if I had seen him yesterday. The expression when the hounds were out, "I dearly love their voices" was word for word from his own lips.' In 1815 classified under 'Sentiment and Reflection'.

This poem received an extraordinary amount of revision in versions later than that of 1798. Hutchinson, p. 232, believed that the object of the alterations was 'to broaden and emphasise the contrast between Simon's radiant youth and decrepit age. In the text of 1798, contrasted traits of youth and age jostle each other throughout the several stanzas i.–vii. . . . in 1832 the traits and evidences of Simon's early vigour are concentrated in stanzas i.–iii., while those of his sad decline are brought together in stanzas vi.–vii., the contrast being marked by the phrase "But oh, the heavy change!" '. De Selincourt, who follows this account, summarizes the changes in order thus ($W.P.W.$, iv. 413; a = ll. 1–4; b = ll. 5–8 of each stanza):

'In 1800, the only change was in 5. l. 2 little *to* dwindled.
'In 1802–15 stanzas 4, 5, 6 are transposed to the order 5, 6, 4.
'In 1820 the order becomes 1*a* 2*b*, 3, 4*a* 5*b*, 6, 5*a* 4*b*, 7, 8, 9.
'In 1827 the order becomes 1*a* 2*b*, 4*a* 3*b*, 3*a* 5*b*, 6, 5*a* 4*b*, 8, 7, 9.
'In 1832 the order becomes 1*a* 2*b*, 3*a* 5*b*, 6, 4*a* 3*b*, *etc.* as 1827.'
For verbal changes see *W.P.W.*, iv. 60–64, 413.

'The object of *Simon Lee* seems to be to vindicate the instinctive character of the emotion of gratitude as against Godwin, who represented it as an unjust and degrading sentiment, having its origin in the unequal distribution of wealth, influence, etc.' (Hutchinson, p. 234).

P. 60. *Anecdote for Fathers.* Composed 1798. I.F.: 'This was suggested in front of Alfoxden. The Boy was a son of my friend Basil Montagu, who had been two or three years under our care. The name of Kilve is from a village on the Bristol Channel, about a mile from Alfoxden; and the name of Liswin Farm was taken from a beautiful spot on the Wye. [The rest of the note concerns John Thelwall, who farmed at Llyswen.].' In 1815 classified under 'Poems referring to the Period of Childhood'.

'Kilve' in the poem corresponds to Racedown, where the Wordsworths lived from 1795 to 1797, and 'Liswyn' to Alfoxden, where they lived from 1797 to 1798. On 7 March 1796 (*E.Y.*, p. 168), Wordsworth wrote to Francis Wrangham: 'Basil is quite well quant au physique mais pour le moral il-y-a bien à craindre. Among other things he lies like a little devil.' In a letter of uncertain date (1825–41) to an unknown correspondent, he wrote: 'In reply to your letter . . . I have to say that my intention was to point out the injurious effects of putting inconsiderate questions to Children, and urging them to give answers upon matters either uninteresting to them, or upon which they had no decided opinion' (*L.Y.*, p. 253). In 1845 the English subtitle (altered to '. . . Practice of Lying . . .' after 1798) was replaced by a Latin motto: 'Retine vim istam, falsa enim dicam, si coges.—EUSEBIUS.'; a Latin version of a Greek hexameter verse cited by Eusebius, *Praeparatio Evangelica*, VI. 5, from Porphyry, as the reply of Apollo to those who attempted to force an oracular answer from him.

P. 63. *We are Seven*. Composed 1798. I.F.: 'Written at Alfoxden in the Spring of 1798, under circumstances somewhat remarkable. The little Girl who is the heroine I met within the area of Goodrich Castle in the year 1793. Having left the Isle of Wight and crost Salisbury Plain as mentioned in the preface to Guilt and Sorrow, I proceeded by Bristol up the Wye, and so on to N. Wales to the Vale of Clwydd, where I spent my summer under the roof of the father of my friend Robert Jones. In reference to this Poem, I will here mention one of the most remarkable facts in my own poetic history and that of Mr. Coleridge. In the Spring of the year 1798, he, my Sister, and myself started from Alfoxden, pretty late in the afternoon, with a view to visit Linton and the Valley of Stones near it, and as our united funds were very small we agreed to defray the expense of the tour by writing a Poem to be sent to the New Monthly Magazine set up by Phillips the Bookseller and edited by Dr. Aikin. Accordingly we set off and proceeded along the Quantock Hills, towards Watchet, and in the course of this walk was planned the Poem of The Ancient Mariner, founded on a dream, as Mr. Coleridge said, of his friend Mr. Cruikshank. Much the greatest part of the story was Mr. Coleridge's invention; but certain parts I myself suggested, for example, some crime was to be committed which should bring upon the Old Navigator, as Coleridge afterwards delighted to call him, the spectral persecution, as a consequence of that crime and his own wanderings. I had been reading in Shelvock's Voyages a day or two before that while doubling Cape Horn they frequently saw Albatrosses in that latitude, the largest sort of seafowl, some extending their wings 12 or 13 feet. "Suppose," said I, "you represent him as having killed one of these birds on entering the South Sea, and that the tutelary Spirits of those regions take upon them to avenge the crime." The incident was thought fit for the purpose and adopted accordingly. I also suggested the navigation of the ship by the dead men, but do not recollect that I had anything more to do with the scheme of the poem. The gloss with which it was subsequently accompanied was not thought of by either of us at the time, at least not a hint of it was given to me, and I have no doubt it was a gratuitous afterthought. We began the composition together on that to me memorable evening. I furnished two or three lines at the beginning of the poem, in particular

> And listened like a three years' child;
> The Mariner had his will.

These trifling contributions all but one (which Mr. C. has with unnecessary scrupulosity recorded) slipt out of his mind as they well might. As we endeavoured to proceed conjointly (I speak of the same evening) our respective manners proved so widely different that it would have been quite presumptuous in me to do anything but separate from an undertaking upon which I could only have been a clog. We returned after a few days from a delightful tour of which I have many pleasant and some of them droll-enough recollections. We returned by Dulverton to Alfoxden. The Ancient Mariner grew and grew till it became too important for our first object which was limited to our expectation of five pounds, and we began to talk of a Volume, which was to consist as Mr. Coleridge has told the world, of Poems chiefly on supernatural subjects [and subjects][1] taken from common life but looked at, as much as might be, through an imaginative medium. Accordingly I wrote The Idiot Boy, Her eyes are wild, &c., We are Seven, The Thorn and some others.—To return to We are Seven, the piece that called forth this note, I composed it while walking in the grove of Alfoxden. My friends will not deem it too trifling to relate that while walking to and fro[2] I composed the last stanza first, having begun with the last line. When it was all but finished, I came in and recited it to Mr. Coleridge and my Sister, and said, "A prefatory stanza must be added, and I should sit down to our little tea-meal with greater pleasure if my task was finished." I mentioned in substance what I wished to be expressed, and Coleridge immediately threw off the stanza thus:

> A little child, dear brother Jem,—

I objected to the rhyme, dear brother Jem as being ludicrous, but we all enjoyed the joke of hitching in our friend James Tobin's name,

---
[1] supernatural subjects taken from common life MS.
[2] walking backward to and fro MS., backward *faintly deleted*.

who was familiarly called Jem. He was the brother of the dramatist, and this reminds me of an anecdote, which it may be worth while here to notice. The said Jem got a sight of the Lyrical Ballads as it was going through the press at Bristol, during which time I was residing in that city. One evening he came to me with a grave face and said, "Wordsworth, I have seen the volume that Coleridge and you are about to publish. There is one poem in it which I earnestly entreat you will cancel, for, if published, it will make you everlastingly ridiculous." I answered that I felt much obliged by the interest he took in my good name as a writer, and begged to know what was the unfortunate piece he alluded to. He said, "It is called We are seven." "Nay," said I, "that shall take its chance however," and he left me in despair. I have only to add that in the spring of 1841 I revisited Goodrich Castle, not having seen that part of the Wye since I met the little girl there in 1793. It would have given me greater pleasure to have found in the neighbouring hamlet traces of one who had interested me so much; but that was impossible, as, unfortunately, I did not even know her name. The ruin, from its position and features, is a most impressive object. I could not but deeply regret that its solemnity was impaired by a fantastic new Castle set up on a projection of the same ridge, as if to shew how far modern art can go in surpassing all that could be done by antiquity and nature with their united graces remembrances and associations. I could have almost wished for power, so much the contrast vexed me, to blow away Sir —— Meyrick's impertinent structure and all the fopperies it contains.'

In 1815 classified under 'Poems referring to the Period of Childhood'. The 'ludicrous' half-line 'dear brother Jim' was removed in the edition of 1815 and did not reappear. The poem, as Wordsworth says in the Preface of 1800, deals with 'the perplexity and obscurity which in childhood attend our notion of death, or rather our utter inability to admit that notion' (p. 158, below). Cf. also: 'Nothing was more difficult for me in childhood than to admit the notion of death as a state applicable to my own being . . . But it was not so much from [feelings] of animal vivacity that *my* difficulty came as from a sense of the indomitableness of the spirit within me' (I.F. note to

Ode: Intimations of Immortality, W.P.W., iv. 463); 'an indisposition [in childhood] to bend to the law of death, as applying to our own particular case' (Wordsworth to Catherine Clarkson, January, 1815; M.Y., ii. 190); 'If we look back upon the days of childhood, we shall find that the time is not in remembrance when, with respect to our own individual Being, the mind was without this assurance [that some part of our nature is imperishable; but this is not to be ascribed to blank ignorance in the child; rather,] the sense of immortality, if not a co-existent and twin birth with Reason, is among the earliest of her offspring' (Essay on Epitaphs, W.P.W., v. 445-6).

P. 65. *Lines written in early Spring*. I.F.: '1798. Actually composed while I was sitting by the side of the brook that runs down from the *Comb*, in which stands the village of Alford, through the grounds of Alfoxden. It was a chosen resort of mine. The brook fell down a sloping rock so as to make a waterfall considerable for that country, and, across the pool below, had fallen a tree, an ash if I rightly remember, from which rose perpendicularly boughs in search of the light intercepted by the deep shade above. The boughs bore leaves of green that for want of sunshine had faded into almost lily-white; and, from the underside of this natural sylvan bridge depended long and beautiful tresses of ivy which waved gently in the breeze that might poetically speaking be called the breath of the waterfall. This motion varied of course in proportion to the power of water in the brook. When with dear friends I revisited this spot, after an interval of more than forty years, this interesting feature of the scene was gone. To the owner of the place I could not but regret that the beauty of this retired part of the grounds had not tempted him to make it more accessible, by a path, not broad or obtrusive, but sufficient for persons who love such scenes to creep along without difficulty.' In 1815 classified under 'Poems proceeding from Sentiment and Reflection.'

P. 66. *The Thorn*. Composed March 1798 (*Journals*, i. 13, cf. i. 16). I.F.: 'Alfoxden. 1798. Arose out of my observing, on the ridge of Quantock Hill, on a stormy day a thorn which I had often passed in calm and bright weather without noticing it. I said to myself, "Cannot I by some invention do as much to make this Thorn

COMMENTARY

[prominently *del.*] an impressive object as the storm has made it to my eyes at this moment." I began the poem accordingly and composed it with great rapidity. Sir George Beaumont painted a picture from it which Wilkie thought his best. He gave it to me; though, when he saw it several times at Rydal Mount afterwards he said, "I could make a better and would like to paint the same subject over again." The sky in this picture is nobly done, but it reminds one too much of Wilson. The only fault however of any consequence is the female figure which is too old and decrepid for one likely to frequent an eminence on such a call.' The quasi-dramatic form is mentioned in Advertisement, 1798, p. 4, above. In *L.B.*, 1800–5, it is discussed in a longer note: 'This Poem ought to have been preceded by an introductory Poem, which I have been prevented from writing by never having felt myself in a mood when it was probable that I should write it well.—The character which I have here introduced speaking is sufficiently common. The Reader will perhaps have a general notion of it, if he has ever known a man, a Captain of a small trading vessel for example, who being past the middle age of life, had retired upon an annuity or small independent income to some village or country town of which he was not a native, or in which he had not been accustomed to live. Such men having little to do become credulous and talkative from indolence; and from the same cause, and other predisposing causes by which it is probable that such men may have been affected, they are prone to superstition. On which account it appeared to me proper to select a character like this to exhibit some of the general laws by which superstition acts upon the mind. Superstitious men are almost always men of slow faculties and deep feelings; their minds are not loose but adhesive; they have a reasonable share of imagination, by which word I mean the faculty which produces impressive effects out of simple elements; but they are utterly destitute of fancy, the power by which pleasure and surprize are excited by sudden varieties of situation and by accumulated imagery.

'It was my wish in this poem to shew the manner in which such men cleave to the same ideas; and to follow the turns of passion, always different, yet not palpably different, by which their conversation is swayed. I had two objects to attain; first, to represent a picture which should not be unimpressive yet consistent with the character that should describe it, secondly, while I adhered to the style in which such persons describe, to take care that words, which in their minds are impregnated with passion, should likewise convey passion to Readers who are not accustomed to sympathize with men feeling in that manner or using such language. It seemed to me that this might be done by calling in the assistance of Lyrical and rapid Metre. It was necessary that the Poem, to be natural, should in reality move slowly; yet I hoped, that, by the aid of the metre, to those who should at all enter into the spirit of the Poem, it would appear to move quickly. The Reader will have the kindness to excuse this note as I am sensible that an introductory Poem is necessary to give this Poem its full effect.

'Upon this occasion I will request permission to add a few words closely connected with THE THORN and many other Poems in these Volumes. There is a numerous class of readers who imagine that the same words cannot be repeated without tautology: this is a great error: virtual tautology is much oftener produced by using different words when the meaning is exactly the same. Words, a Poet's words more particularly, ought to be weighed in the balance of feeling and not measured by the space which they occupy upon paper. For the Reader cannot be too often reminded that Poetry is passion: it is the history or science of feelings: now every man must know that an attempt is rarely made to communicate impassioned feelings without something of an accompanying consciousness of the inadequateness of our own powers, or the deficiencies of language. During such efforts there will be a craving in the mind, and as long as it is unsatisfied the Speaker will cling to the same words, or words of the same character. There are also various other reasons why repetition and apparent tautology are frequently beauties of the highest kind. Among the chief of these reasons is the interest which the mind attaches to words, not only as symbols of the passion, but as *things*, active and efficient, which are of themselves part of the passion. And further, from a spirit of fondness, exultation, and gratitude, the mind luxuriates in the repetition of words which appear successfully

COMMENTARY 141

to communicate its feelings. The truth of these remarks might be shewn by innumerable passages from the Bible and from the impassioned poetry of every nation.

'"Awake, awake Deborah: awake, awake, utter a song: Arise Barak, and lead thy captivity captive, thou Son of Abinoam.

'"At her feet he bowed, he fell, he lay down: at her feet he bowed, he fell; where he bowed there he fell down dead.

'"Why is his Chariot so long in coming? Why tarry the Wheels of his Chariot?"—Judges, Chap. 5th. Verses 12th, 27th, and part of 28th.—See also the whole of that tumultuous and wonderful Poem.'

In 1815 classified under 'Poems of the Imagination', whether for the reason given for *Goody Blake* (see note to p. 50, above) or because Wordsworth thought the poem 'produced by' his own imagination is not clear. Whatever the reason, the poem remained under this heading in later editions. Apart from the scenic inspiration claimed by Wordsworth in I.F., two literary sources have been proposed: the translation (*The Lass of Fair Wone*) by William Taylor of Bürger's *Des Pfarrers Tochter von Taubenheim* in *Monthly Magazine*, i (1796), 223–4, and in other magazines; and a Scottish ballad on a similar theme which Wordsworth copied into his Commonplace Book. The theme of the deserted mother is, however, commonplace in the late eighteenth century; see Introd., sec. IV. A version of the early lines in the Alfoxden MS. shows that Wordsworth began to write in octosyllabic couplets (*W.P.W.*, ii. 240).

116. Martha Ray] The editors wonder at Wordsworth's obtuseness in using this, the name of his friend Basil Montagu's mother, mistress of the fourth Earl of Sandwich. She was murdered by a disappointed lover in 1779.

P. 76. *The Last of the Flock.* Composed 1798. I.F.: 'Produced at the same time, and for the same purpose [as *The Complaint of a Forsaken Indian Woman*, i.e. for *L.B.*]. The incident occurred in the village of Holford, close by Alfoxden.' In 1815 classified under 'Poems founded on the Affections'. A defence of the instinctive feeling for property; no doubt, as the critics suggest, in opposition to Godwin's view of property as a social evil. The shepherd regards his flock as just as valuable to him as his family (81–90). In 1836 Wordsworth justified the word 'alone' in l. 4: 'Funerals . . . we have all attended, and most of us must have seen then weeping in the public roads . . . I was a witness to a sight of this kind the other day in the Streets of Kendal. . . . But for my own part, notwithstanding what has here been said in verse, I never in my whole life saw a man weep *alone* in the roads; but a friend of mine *did* see this poor man weeping *alone*, with the Lamb, the last of his flock, in his arms' (Wordsworth to John Kenyon, Autumn 1836; *L.Y.*, p. 812).

P. 80. *The Dungeon*. An extract from Coleridge's *Osorio*; see note to *The Foster-Mother's Tale*, p. 126, above; and *C.P.W.*, ii. 586–7.

23. breathing sweets] John Philips, *Cyder*, II. 57–58: '*English* Plains Blush with pomaceous Harvests, breathing Sweets'.

P. 81. *The Mad Mother*. I.F.: 'Alfoxden, 1798. The subject was reported to me by a Lady of Bristol who had seen the poor creature.' In 1815 classified under 'Poems founded on the Affections'. The title was dropped in 1815 in favour of the first line of the poem. Concerned with 'tracing the maternal passion through . . . its more subtle windings', Preface of 1800, p. 158, below; i.e. demonstrating the persistence, even during the mental derangement of the mother, of this one of 'the great and simple affections of our nature'.

In the letter to Kenyon cited above (note to *The Last of the Flock*), Wordsworth defends l. 10: 'And it was in the English tongue', on the ground that 'though she came from far [cf. l. 4], English was her native tongue—which shows her either to be of these Islands, or a North American. On the latter supposition, while the distance removes her from us, the fact of her speaking our language brings us at once into close sympathy with her' (*L.Y.*, pp. 812–13).

Hutchinson, p. 245, proposed the influence of *Lady Anne Bothwell's Lament*, in Percy's *Reliques*. The themes are similar, and there are some verbal resemblances: *Lament*, 5: 'Balow, my boy, thy mothers joy', cf. *Mad Mother*, 41–42; *Lament*, 13–14: 'But now I see, most cruell hee Cares neither for my babe nor mee', cf. *Mad Mother*, 61; *Lament*, 16: 'when thou wakest, sweitly smile', cf. *Mad Mother*, 91; *Lament*, 34: 'Thy winsome smiles maun eise my paine', cf. *Mad Mother*, 33–34; *Lament*, 35: 'My babe and I'll together live', cf. *Mad Mother*,

74, 100; *Lament*, 37: 'My babe and I right saft will ly', cf. *Mad Mother*, 55–56.

39–40. Cited by Coleridge (*C.N.B.*, ii. 2112) as an instance of the working of the Imagination: 'In the men of continuous and discontinuous minds explain & demonstrate the vast difference between the disjunction conjunctive of the sudden Images *seized* on from external Contingents by Passion & Imagination (which is Passion eagle-eyed)—The Breeze I see, is in the Tree—It comes to cool my Babe and me.—which is the property & prerogative of continuous minds of the highest order, & the conjunction disjunctive of Wit ...' In *Biog. Lit.*, ii. 123, Coleridge describes the lines as 'so expressive of that deranged state, in which from the increased sensibility the sufferer's attention is abruptly drawn off by every trifle, and in the same instant plucked back again by the one despotic thought, bringing home with it, by the blending, *fusing* power of Imagination and Passion, the alien object to which it had been so abruptly diverted, no longer an alien but an ally and an inmate.'

P. 84. *The Idiot Boy*. I.F.: 'Alfoxden, 1798. The last stanza, "The Cocks did crow, And the sun did shine so cold", was the foundation of the whole. The words were reported to me by my dear friend, Thomas Poole; but I have since heard the same repeated of other Idiots. Let me add that this long poem was composed in the groves of Alfoxden almost extempore; not a word, I believe, being corrected, though one stanza was omitted. I mention this in gratitude to those happy moments, for, in truth, I never wrote anything with so much glee.' In 1815 classified under 'Poems founded on the Affections'. Described in the Preface of 1800 as dealing with 'the maternal passion' in 'its more subtle windings' (p. 158, below); cf. note to *The Mad Mother*, p. 142, above. This poem shows 'the maternal passion' exercised upon, and persisting in spite of, an abnormal object.

The Idiot Boy was the subject of a notable letter of 1802 to Wordsworth written by John Wilson ('Christopher North'), who criticizes the poem on the ground that events common in human experience are not *ipso facto* suitable material for poetry: 'many feelings which are undoubtedly natural ... are improper subjects for poetry. ... There are a thousand occurrences happening every day which do not in the least interest an unconcerned spectator, though they no doubt occasion various emotions in the breast of those to whom they immediately relate. To describe these in poetry would be improper' (Elsie Smith, *An Estimate of William Wordsworth by his Contemporaries*, Oxford, 1932, p. 56). Wordsworth justifies the poem in a well-known reply urging that 'It is not enough for me as a poet, to delineate merely such feelings as all men *do* sympathise with but, it is also highly desirable to add to these others, such as all men *may* sympathize with, and such as there is reason to believe they would be better and more moral beings if they did sympathize with' (*E.Y.*, p. 358).

P. 101. *Lines written near Richmond.* Composed 1789. In *L.B.*, 1800, divided into two poems, *Lines written while Sailing in a Boat at Evening* (sts. 1–2 of the present poem), and *Remembrance of Collins composed upon the Thames near Richmond* (sts. 3–5). I.F.: 'This title is scarcely correct. It was during a solitary walk on the banks of the Cam that I was first struck with this appearance, and applied it to my own feelings in the manner here expressed, changing the scene to the Thames, near Windsor. This, and the three stanzas of the following poem, "Remembrance of Collins" formed one piece; but, upon the recommendation of Coleridge, the three last stanzas were separated from the other.'

In 1815 classified under 'Poems proceeding from Sentiment and Reflection'; in 1845 transferred to 'Poems written in Youth'.

17. Cf. *The River Duddon*, Sonnet XXXIV. 5: 'Still glides the Stream, and shall for ever glide'.

29. Hutchinson, contrasting 'once' here and '*later*' in 30, asserts that 29 refers to Collins's *Ode on the Poetical Character*; but I can find no passage in Collins's Ode parallel to what Wordsworth says here.

30. here] On or beside the Thames. St. 4 of Collins's *Ode on the Death of Mr. Thomson* (James Thomson [1700–48], author of *The Seasons*), which is quoted by Wordsworth in his final stanza, reads:

> Remembrance oft shall haunt the shore
>   When Thames in summer wreaths is drest,
> And oft suspend the dashing oar
>   To bid his gentle spirit rest!

COMMENTARY

Thomson was buried in Richmond Church.
31–32. Collins, *Ode on the Death of Mr. Thomson*, sts. 3, 6:

> Then maids and youths shall linger here ...
> Shall sadly seem in Pity's ear
> To hear the Woodland Pilgrim's knell.

> But Thou, who own'st that earthly bed,
> Ah! what will every dirge avail?
> Or tears, which Love and Pity shed ... ?

P. 103. *Expostulation and Reply*. I.F.: 'This poem is a favourite among the Quakers, as I have learnt on many occasions. It was composed in front of the house at Alfoxden in the spring of 1798.' In 1815 classified under 'Poems proceeding from Sentiment and Reflection'. Referred to in Advertisement, p. 4, above. The 'friend ... attached to modern books of Moral Philosophy' is commonly said to be William Hazlitt, who visited Wordsworth at Alfoxden in May–June 1798. See Hazlitt's 'My First Acquaintance with Poets', in *Works*, ed. Howe (London, 1930–4), xvii. 116 ff., especially p. 119: 'I got into a metaphysical argument with Wordsworth, while Coleridge was explaining the different notes of the nightingale to his sister, in which we neither of us succeeded in making ourselves perfectly clear and intelligible.' In 'A Reply to "Z"' (*Works*, ix. 4), Hazlitt says that when he 'once explained the argument of that Essay ["On the Principles of Human Action", in progress in 1798] to Mr. Wordsworth (and it is a hard matter to explain any thing to him) I remember he said he thought there was something in it, but it was what every shoemaker must have thought of'. It is clear that Hazlitt and Wordsworth discussed philosophical principles in 1798, but hardly certain that this poem refers to him.

15. Matthew] Commonly identified with William Taylor, Wordsworth's master at Hawkshead Grammar School; Mrs. Moorman, *Early Years*, p. 52, suggests that he is, rather, the packman who was Wordsworth's model for the Wanderer in *The Excursion*. Whichever identification may be correct, the mention of Esthwaite in 13 indicates that Wordsworth is transferring the scene to the region

of his schooldays, whether or not the debate was suggested by talk with Hazlitt. In the I.F. note to *Matthew* (*W.P.W.*, iv. 415), Wordsworth says that 'this Schoolmaster was made up of several both of his class and men of other occupations'.

P. 104. *The Tables Turned.* I.F.: 'Composed at the same time [as the preceding poem].' In 1815 classified under 'Poems proceeding from Sentiment and Reflection'.

26–32. Cf. *Prel.* (1805), XI. 123 ff.:

> There comes a time when Reason . . .
>   that humbler power
> Which carries on its no inglorious work
> By logic and minute analysis
> Is of all Idols that which pleases most
> The growing mind . . .
>   danger cannot but attend
> Upon a Function rather proud to be
> The enemy of falsehood, than the friend
> Of truth, to sit in judgment than to feel.
> Oh! soul of Nature . . .
>   with whom I too
> Rejoiced, through early youth before the winds
> And powerful waters, and in lights and shades
> That march'd and countermarch'd about the hills
> In glorious apparition, now all eye
> And now all ear; but ever with the heart
> Employ'd, and the majestic intellect.

In a late version of a nearby passage, *Prel.* (1850), XII. 88 ff., Wordsworth speaks of scanning 'the visible Universe . . . with microscopic view'. Hutchinson (p. 251) compares the account of John Wordsworth in 'When to the attractions', 80 ff. (*W.P.W.*, ii. 122):

> from the solitude
> Of the vast sea didst bring a watchful heart

COMMENTARY

Still couchant, an inevitable ear,
And an eye practised like a blind man's touch.

P. 105. *Old Man Travelling*. Composed 1797. I.F.: 'If I recollect right these verses were an overflowing from the old Cumberland Beggar.' In 1815 classified under 'Poems referring to the Period of Old Age'. The first three words of the present title were omitted in 1800 and later editions, and in 1845 the words 'A Sketch' were also dropped. Ll. 15–20 were dropped in 1815 and thereafter. Versions of the poem appear in the same MSS. as contain *The Old Cumberland Beggar*; see *W.P.W.*, iv. 234–40, 247.

The poem might serve as an instance of the successful use in verse of 'the language of prose' which is canvassed in the Preface of 1800 (pp. 162–4, below): the vocabulary and syntax are of the utmost simplicity, yet convey, by understatement or oblique statement (1–2), and by physical or intellectual complexity presented as a paradoxical unity (3–4, 6–7, 11–12), the most acute and purposeful observation on the part of the poet.

P. 106. *The Complaint of a Forsaken Indian Woman*. I.F.: 'Written at Alfoxden, in 1798, where I read Hearne's Journey with deep interest. It was composed for the volume of Lyrical Ballads.' Designed to 'follow the fluxes and refluxes of the mind when agitated by the great and simple affections of our nature . . . by accompanying the last struggles of a human being at the approach of death, cleaving in solitude to life and society' (Preface of 1800, p. 158, below). The introductory note, but very little of the poem, is adapted verbally from Samuel Hearne, *A Journey from Prince of Wales's Fort in Hudson's Bay to the Northern Ocean* (London, 1795), ed. J. B. Tyrrell (Toronto, 1911), pp. 218–19: 'One of the Indian's wives, who for some time had been in a consumption, had for a few days past become so weak as to be incapable of travelling, which, among those people, is the most deplorable state to which a human being can possibly be brought. Whether she had been given over by the doctors, or that it was for want of friends among them, I cannot tell, but certain it is, that no expedients were taken for her recovery; so that, without much ceremony, she was left unassisted, to perish above-ground.

COMMENTARY

'Though this was the first instance of the kind I had seen, it is the common, and indeed the constant practice of those Indians; for when a grown person is so ill, especially in the Summer, as not to be able to walk, and too heavy to be carried, they say it is better to leave one who is past recovery, than for the whole family to sit down by them and starve to death; well knowing that they cannot be of any service to the afflicted. On those occasions, therefore, the friends or relations of the sick generally leave them some victuals and water; and, if the situation of the place will afford it, a little firing. When those articles are provided, the person to be left is acquainted with the road which the others intend to go ; and then, after covering them well up with deer skins, &c. they take their leave, and walk away crying.

'Sometimes persons left thus, recover; and come up with their friends, or wander about till they meet with other Indians, whom they accompany till they again join their relations. Instances of this kind are seldom known. The poor woman above mentioned, however, came up with us three several times, after having been left in the manner described. At length, poor creature! she dropt behind, and no one attempted to go back in search of her.

'A custom apparently so unnatural is perhaps not to be found among any other of the human race: if properly considered, however, it may with justice be ascribed to necessity and self-preservation, rather than to the want of humanity and social feeling, which ought to be the characteristic of men, as the noblest part of the creation. Necessity, added to national custom, contributes principally to make scenes of this kind less shocking to those people, than they must appear to the more civilized part of mankind.'

Ibid., p. 235: 'I do not remember to have met with any travellers into high Northern latitudes, who remarked their having heard the Northern Lights make any noise in the air as they vary their colours or position; which may probably be owing to the want of perfect silence at the time they made their observations on those meteors. I can positively affirm, that in still nights I have frequently heard them make a rustling and crackling noise, like the waving of a large flag in a fresh gale of wind.'

P. 109. *The Convict.* Date of composition unknown; 1793 is

COMMENTARY 149

suggested by editors on the basis of the 'Godwinian humanitarianism' (de Selincourt) of the poem. First published in the *Morning Post*, 14 December 1797, with some variant readings, and never reprinted by Wordsworth after *L.B.*, 1798. In the *Morning Post* it appears over the signature 'Mortimer', the name given to the hero (subsequently called Marmaduke) of Wordsworth's play *The Borderers*. Wordsworth was in London on 13 December 1797, trying, without success, to have *The Borderers* staged; he proposed to leave London for Bristol on 15 December (*E.Y.*, p. 196). Presumably he arranged for the publication of the poem during this visit.

Emile Legouis, *The Early Life of William Wordsworth* (London, 1897), p. 369, observes that the last stanza refers to Godwin's proposal that transportation to colonies should replace the death penalty.

P. 111. *Lines written a few miles above Tintern Abbey.* I.F.: 'July 1798. No poem of mine was composed under circumstances more pleasant for me to remember than this. I began it upon leaving Tintern, after crossing the Wye, and concluded it just as I was entering Bristol in the evening, after a ramble of 4 or 5 days, with my sister. Not a line of it was altered, and not any part of it written down till I reached Bristol. It was published almost immediately after in the little volume of which so much has been said in these notes. (The Lyrical Ballads, as first published at Bristol by Cottle).' In 1815 classified under 'Poems of the Imagination'. In *L.B.*, 1800, Wordsworth added the following: 'NOTE to the Poem ON REVISITING THE WYE... I have not ventured to call this Poem an Ode; but it was written with a hope that in the transitions, and the impassioned music of the versification would be found the principal requisites of that species of composition.'

Wordsworth's statement that 'Not a line of [the poem] was altered', which seems to imply (though it need not) that at least the text of 1798 reproduces the poem as it was orally composed during the walk, is not wholly credible in view of the line cancelled after l. 19 of the present text (see note to 19, below), which looks like a survival in MS. copy of an earlier version. There are verbal borrowings which might suggest the use of books (see especially note on 7–19, below). In *N. & Q.*, cxcvi (1951), 209–10, I pointed out that at least one

COMMENTARY

fragment of comparable date (*W.P.W.*, v. 341, fragment vi) could be inserted into the present text after 'To blow against thee' (138);[1] this might suggest that the fragment comprises lines (*a*) rejected from this poem, or (*b*) rejected from a poem addressed to Dorothy Wordsworth upon which Wordsworth drew for the later part of *Tintern Abbey*, or (*c*) written for insertion into *Tintern Abbey* or a poem such as that suggested in (*b*).

1. Five years have passed] Wordsworth visited the Wye Valley in August 1793, in the course of his tour from the Isle of Wight to North Wales. He and Dorothy Wordsworth walked up and down the Wye Valley between 9 and 13 July 1798 (Moorman, *Early Years*, p. 401).

7–19. Mrs. Moorman (*Early Years*, p. 402) compares a passage in William Gilpin's *Observations on the River Wye* (third ed., 1792, p. 22): 'Many of the furnaces, on the banks of the river, consume charcoal, which is manufactured on the spot; and the smoke, which is frequently seen issuing from the sides of the hills; and spreading it's thin veil over a part of them, beautifully breaks their lines, and unites them with the sky.' She suggests that Wordsworth may have had Gilpin's book with him during the tour of 1798.

19. After this line *L.B.*, 1798, prints the line: 'And the low copses —coming from the trees'. The Errata of 1798 cancels the line, which is therefore omitted from the present text.

34. De Selincourt compares Milton, *The Judgment of Martin Bucer, concerning Divorce*, Preface: '. . . imprudent canons: whereby good men in the best portion of their lives . . . are compelled to civil indignities, which by the law of Moses bad men were not compelled to'.

42–50. This trance-like state seems to be the same as that which Wordsworth on various occasions describes as one in which the

---

[1] And let the misty mountain winds be free
  To blow against thee: [and beneath the star
  Of evening let the steep and lonely path,
  The steep path of the rocky mountain side
  Among the stillness of the mountains hear
  The panting of thy breath;] in after years, &c.

distinction between the individual and the world outside him appears to be lost; see, for instance, *Prel.* (1805), II. 367–71:

> Oft in these moments such a holy calm
> Did overspread my soul, that I forgot
> That I had bodily eyes, and what I saw
> Appear'd like something in myself, a dream,
> A prospect in my mind;

I.F. note to *Ode: Intimations of Immortality* (*W.P.W.*, iv. 463): 'I was often [in childhood] unable to think of external things as having external existence, and I communed with all that I saw as something not apart from, but inherent in, my own immaterial nature.'

53–54. A half-reminiscence of *Macbeth*, III. ii. 23: 'After life's fitful fever he sleeps well', with, perhaps, a suggestion of *Hamlet*, I. ii. 133–4: 'How . . . unprofitable Seem to me all the uses of this world!'

67–84. Wordsworth so describes his reaction to nature at this time in *Prel.* (1805), XI. 186–95:

> my delights
> . . . were sought insatiably,
> Though 'twas a transport of the outward sense,
> Not of the mind, vivid but not profound:
> Yet was I often greedy in the chace,
> And roam'd from hill to hill, from rock to rock,
> Still craving combinations of new forms,
> New pleasure, wider empire for the sight,
> Proud of its own endowments, and rejoiced
> To lay the inner faculties asleep.

Cf. also *To the Daisy* (*W.P.W.*, ii. 135), 1–4:

> In youth from rock to rock I went,
> From hill to hill in discontent
> Of pleasure high and turbulent,
> Most pleased when most uneasy.

74–75. See the episodes of swimming, bird-snaring, bird-nesting,

the stolen boat, and skating, described in *Prel.* (1805), I. 291–489.
107, and footnote. Wordsworth refers to Edward Young, *Night Thoughts*, VI. 424: 'And half-create the wondrous world they [the senses] see'. Cf. *W.P.W.*, v. 340, Fragment I:

> I hear thy voice,
> Beloved Derwent, that peculiar voice
> Heard in the stillness of the evening air,
> Half-heard and half-created;

p. 343, Fragment IV. vi:

> There is creation in the eye,
> Nor less in all the other senses; powers
> They are that colour, model, and combine
> The things perceived with such an absolute
> Essential energy that we may say
> That those most godlike faculties of ours
> At one and the same moment are the mind
> And the mind's minister;

p. 344, Fragment IV. vii: 'the godlike senses'.
111. Cf. Akenside, *Pleasures of Imagination* (1744), I. 21–23:

> with thee [Harmony] comes
> The guide, the guardian of their lovely sports,
> Majestic Truth

('. . . of their mystic rites, Wise Order', edition of 1757).
129. evil tongues] Milton, *Paradise Lost*, VII. 25–26: 'though fall'n on evil dayes, On evil dayes though fall'n, and evil tongues.'

Appendix

WORDSWORTH'S PREFACE OF 1800, WITH A COLLATION OF THE ENLARGED PREFACE OF 1802

PREFACE. [1800]

THE first Volume of these Poems has already been submitted to general perusal. It was published, as an experiment[1] which, I hoped, might be of some use to ascertain, how far, by fitting to metrical arrangement a selection of the real language of men in a state of vivid sensation, that sort of pleasure and that quantity of pleasure may be imparted, which a Poet may rationally endeavour to impart.

I had formed no very inaccurate estimate of the probable effect of those Poems: I flattered myself that they who should be pleased with them would read them with more than common pleasure: and[1] on the other hand[1] I was well aware[1] that by those who should dislike them they would be read with more than common dislike. The result has differed from my expectation in this only, that I have pleased a greater number, than I ventured to hope I should please.

For the sake of variety[1] and from a consciousness of my own weakness[1] I was induced to request the assistance of a Friend, who furnished me with the Poems of the ANCIENT MARINER, the FOSTER-MOTHER'S TALE, the NIGHTINGALE, the DUNGEON,[1a] and the Poem entitled LOVE. I should not, however, have requested this assistance, had I not believed that the poems[2] of my Friend would in a great measure have the same tendency as my own, and that,[2a] though there would be found a difference, there would be found no discordance in

---

[1] 1802: experiment, . . . and, . . . hand, . . . aware, . . . variety, . . . weakness,

[1a] 1802 *omits* the DUNGEON,

[2] 1802: Poems

[2a] *The reading of this paragraph, down to* my own, and that, *given above, is that of most copies of* Lyrical Ballads, *1800: it is the reading of a cancel-page vi in that edition. In three known copies the page is uncancelled and reads:* For the sake of variety and from a consciousness of my own

NLB

the colours of our style; as our opinions on the subject of poetry do almost entirely coincide.

Several of my Friends are anxious for the success of these Poems from a belief, that[3] if the views, with which they were composed, were indeed realized, a class of Poetry would be produced, well adapted to interest mankind permanently, and not unimportant in the multiplicity[3] and in the quality of its moral relations: and on this account they have advised me to prefix a systematic defence of the theory, upon which the poems were written. But I was unwilling to undertake the task, because I knew that on this occasion the Reader would look coldly upon my arguments, since I might be suspected of having been principally influenced by the selfish and foolish hope of *reasoning* him into an approbation of these particular Poems: and I was still more unwilling to undertake the task, because[4] adequately to display my opinions[4] and fully to enforce my arguments[4] would require a space wholly disproportionate to the nature of a preface. For to treat the subject with the clearness and coherence, of which I believe it susceptible, it would be necessary to give a full account of the present state of the public taste in this country, and to determine how far this taste is healthy or depraved; which[5] again could not be determined, without pointing out, in what manner language and the human mind act and react on each other, and without retracing the revolutions not of literature alone[5] but

weakness I have again requested the assistance of a Friend who contributed largely to the first volume,* and who has now furnished me with the Poem of Christabel, without which I should not yet have ventured to present a second volume to the public. I should not however have requested this assistance, had I not believed that the poems of my Friend would in a great measure have the same tendency as my own, and that,

---

* The Poems supplied by my Friend, are the ANTIENT MARINER, the FOSTER-MOTHER'S TALE, the NIGHTINGALE, the DUNGEON, and the Poem entitled, LOVE. *The uncancelled reading represents an intention, abandoned in October 1800, to include Coleridge's* Christabel *in* Lyrical Ballads, *1800.*

[3] 1802: that, if the views with which they were composed were . . . multiplicity, and

[4] 1802: because, . . . opinions, . . . arguments,

[5] 1802: which, again, . . . re-act . . . revolutions, . . . alone,

APPENDIX 155

likewise of society itself. I have therefore altogether declined to enter regularly upon this defence; yet I am sensible, that there would be some impropriety in abruptly obtruding upon the Public, without a few words of introduction, Poems so materially different from those, upon which general approbation is at present bestowed.

It is supposed, that by the act of writing in verse an Author makes a formal engagement that he will gratify certain known habits of association,[6] that he not only thus apprizes the Reader that certain classes of ideas and expressions will be found in his book, but that others will be carefully excluded. This exponent or symbol held forth by metrical language must in different æras of literature have excited very different expectations: for example, in the age of Catullus Terence and Lucretia, and that of Statius or Claudian,[7] and in our own country, in the age of Shakespeare and Beaumont and Fletcher, and that of Donne and Cowley, or Dryden, or Pope. I will not take upon me to determine the exact import of the promise which by the act of writing in verse an Author in the present day[8] makes to his Reader; but I am certain[8] it will appear to many persons that I have not fulfilled the terms of an engagement thus voluntarily contracted.[9] I hope therefore the Reader will not censure me, if I attempt to state what I have proposed to myself to perform,[9] and also, (as far as the limits of a preface will permit) to explain some of the chief reasons which have determined me in the choice of my purpose: that at least he may be spared any unpleasant feeling of disappointment, and that I myself may be protected from the most dishonorable accusation which can be brought against an Author, namely, that of an indolence

[6] 1802: association;

[7] 1802: Catullus, Terence, and Lucretius [*also corrected in Errata of 1800*] and . . . Claudian;

[8] 1802: Author, . . . day, . . . certain,

[9] 1802 inserts (from 1798) after 'contracted.': They who have been accustomed to the gaudiness and inane phraseology of many modern writers, if they persist in reading this book to its conclusion, will, no doubt, frequently have to struggle with feelings of strangeness and aukwardness: they will look round for poetry, and will be induced to inquire by what species of courtesy these attempts can be permitted to assume that title. . . . perform;

APPENDIX

which prevents him from endeavouring to ascertain what is his duty, or, when his duty is ascertained[10] prevents him from performing it.

The principal object then[10] which I proposed to myself in these Poems was to make the incidents of common life interesting[11] by tracing in them, truly though not ostentatiously, the primary laws of our nature: chiefly[11a] as far as regards the manner in which we associate ideas in a state of excitement. Low and rustic life was generally chosen because in that situation[12] the essential passions of the heart find a better soil in which they can attain their maturity, are less under restraint, and speak a plainer and more emphatic language; because in that situation[13] our elementary feelings exist[13] in a state of greater simplicity and consequently[13] may be more accurately contemplated and more forcibly communicated; because the manners of rural life germinate from those elementary feelings; and from[13] the necessary character of rural occupations[13] are more easily comprehended; and are more durable; and lastly, because in that situation[14] the passions of men are incorporated with the beautiful and permanent forms of nature. The language too[14] of these men is adopted (purified indeed from what appear to be its real defects, from all lasting and rational causes of dislike or disgust) because such men hourly communicate with the best objects from which the best part of language is originally derived; and because, from their rank in society and the sameness and narrow circle of their intercourse, being less under the action[15] of social vanity they convey their feelings and notions in

[10] 1802: ascertained, ... object, then,

[11] 1802 changes 'to make the incidents ... interesting' to: to chuse incidents and situations from common life, and to relate or describe them, throughout, as far as was possible, in a selection of language really used by men; and, at the same time, to throw over them a certain colouring of imagination, whereby ordinary things should be presented to the mind in an unusual way; and, further, and above all, to make these incidents and situations interesting

[11a] 1802: chiefly,

[12] 1802: chosen, because in that condition, the

[13] 1802: because in that condition of life ... co-exist ... simplicity, and, consequently, ... contemplated, ... and, from ... occupations,

[14] 1802: condition ... language, too,

[15] 1802: influence

APPENDIX 157

simple and unelaborated expressions. Accordingly[16] such a language arising out of repeated experience and regular feelings is a more permanent and a far more philosophical language than that which is frequently substituted for it by Poets, who think that they are conferring honour upon themselves and their art in proportion as they separate themselves from the sympathies of men, and indulge in arbitrary and capricious habits of expression in order to furnish food for fickle tastes and fickle appetites[16] of their own creation.*

I cannot[17] be insensible of the present outcry against the triviality and meanness both of thought and language, which some of my contemporaries have occasionally introduced into their metrical compositions; and I acknowledge[17] that this defect where it exists, is more dishonorable to the Writer's own character than false refinement or arbitrary innovation, though I should contend at the same time that it is far less pernicious in the sum of its consequences. From such verses the Poems in these volumes will be found distinguished at least by one mark of difference, that each of them has a worthy *purpose*. Not that I mean to say, that I always began to write with a distinct purpose formally conceived; but I believe that my habits of meditation have so formed my feelings, as that my descriptions of such objects as strongly excite those feelings, will be found to carry along with them a *purpose*. If in this opinion I am mistaken[18] I can have little right to the name of a Poet. For all good poetry is the spontaneous overflow of powerful feelings;[18] but though this be true, Poems to which any value can be attached, were never produced on any variety of subjects but by a man who[19] being possessed of more than usual organic sensibility had also thought long and deeply. For our continued influxes of feeling are modified and directed by our thoughts, which are indeed the representatives of all our past

---

* It is worth while here to observe that the affecting parts of Chaucer are almost always expressed in language pure and universally intelligible even to this day.

[16] 1802: Accordingly, such a language, . . . feelings, . . . permanent, . . . language, . . . and their art, . . . expression, . . . tastes, and fickle appetites,

[17] 1802: I cannot, however, . . . acknowledge, that this defect,

[18] 1802: mistaken, . . . feelings:

[19] 1802: a man, who . . . sensibility, had

feelings; and as by contemplating the relation of these general representatives[20] to each other, we discover what is really important to men, so by the repetition and continuance of this act feelings connected with important subjects[20] will be nourished, till at length, if we be originally possessed of much organic sensibility, such habits of mind will be produced that by obeying blindly and mechanically the impulses of those habits we shall describe objects and utter sentiments of such a nature and in such connection with each other, that the understanding of the being to whom we address ourselves, if he be in a healthful state of association, must necessarily be in some degree enlightened, his taste exalted, and his affections ameliorated.[20]

I have said that each of these poems has a purpose. I have also informed my Reader what this purpose will be found principally to be: namely to illustrate the manner in which our feelings and ideas are associated in a state of excitement. But speaking in less general language,[21] it is to follow the fluxes and refluxes of the mind when agitated by the great and simple affections of our nature. This object I have endeavoured in these short essays to attain by various means; by tracing the maternal passion through many of its more subtle windings, as in the poems of the IDIOT BOY and the MAD MOTHER; by accompanying the last struggles of a human being[22] at the approach of death, cleaving in solitude to life and society, as in the Poem of the FORSAKEN INDIAN; by shewing, as in the Stanzas entitled WE ARE SEVEN,[23] the perplexity and obscurity which in childhood attend our notion of death, or rather our utter inability to admit that notion; or by displaying the strength of fraternal, or to speak more philosophically, of moral attachment when early associated with the great and beautiful objects of nature, as in THE BROTHERS; or, as in the Incident of SIMON LEE, by placing my Reader in the way of receiving

[20] 1802: and, . . . representatives to each other we discover what is really important to men, so, . . . this act, our feelings will be connected . . . subjects, till at length, if we be originally possessed of much sensibility, . . . produced, that, by . . . habits, . . . objects, and utter sentiments, . . . in some degree enlightened, and his affections ameliorated.

[21] 1802: But, speaking in language somewhat more appropriate,

[22] 1802: human being, at the

[23] 1802: SEVEN

APPENDIX 159

from ordinary moral sensations another and more salutary impression than we are accustomed to receive from them. It has also been part of my general purpose to attempt to sketch characters under the influence of less impassioned feelings, as in[24] the OLD MAN TRAVELLING, THE TWO THIEVES, &c. characters of which the elements are simple, belonging rather to nature than to manners, such as exist now[25] and will probably always exist, and which from their constitution may be distinctly and profitably contemplated. I will not abuse the indulgence of my Reader by dwelling longer upon this subject; but it is proper that I should mention one other circumstance which distinguishes these Poems from the popular Poetry of the day; it is this, that the feeling therein developed gives importance to the action and situation[26] and not the action and situation to the feeling. My meaning will be rendered perfectly intelligible by referring my Reader to the Poems entitled POOR SUSAN and the CHILDLESS FATHER, particularly to the last Stanza of the latter Poem.

I will not suffer a sense of false modesty to prevent me from asserting, that I point my Reader's attention to this mark of distinction far[26] less for the sake of these particular Poems than from the general importance of the subject. The subject is indeed important! For the human mind is capable of excitement[27] without the application of gross and violent stimulants; and he must have a very faint perception of its beauty and dignity who does not know this, and who does not further know that[28] one being is elevated above another in proportion as he possesses this capability. It has therefore appeared to me[29] that to endeavour to produce or enlarge this capability is one of the best services in which, at any period, a Writer can be engaged; but this service, excellent at all times, is especially so at the present day. For a multitude of causes unknown to former times[30] are now

[24] 1802: feelings, as in the TWO APRIL MORNINGS, THE FOUNTAIN, THE
[25] 1802: exist now, and
[26] 1802: situation, . . . distinction, far
[27] 1802: of being excited
[28] 1802: know, that . . . another, in
[29] 1802: appeared to me, that
[30] 1802: causes, . . . times, are

acting with a combined force to blunt the discriminating powers of the mind, and unfitting it for all voluntary exertion to reduce it to a state of almost savage torpor. The most effective of these causes are the great national events which are daily taking place, and the encreasing accumulation of men in cities, where the uniformity of their occupations produces a craving for extraordinary incident[31] which the rapid communication of intelligence hourly gratifies. To this tendency of life and manners the literature and theatrical exhibitions of the country have conformed themselves. The invaluable works of our elder writers, I had almost said the works of Shakespear and Milton, are driven into neglect by frantic novels, sickly and stupid German Tragedies, and deluges of idle and extravagant stories in verse.— When I think upon this degrading thirst after outrageous stimulation[32] I am almost ashamed to have spoken of the feeble effort with which I have endeavoured to counteract it; and[33] reflecting upon the magnitude of the general evil, I should be oppressed with no dishonorable melancholy, had I not a deep impression of certain inherent and indestructible qualities of the human mind, and likewise of certain powers in the great and permanent objects that act upon it which are equally inherent and indestructible; and did I not further add to this impression a belief[34] that the time is approaching when the evil will be systematically opposed by men of greater powers and with far more distinguished success.[35]

Having dwelt thus long on the subjects and aim of these Poems, I shall request the Reader's permission to apprize him of a few circumstances relating to their *style*, in order, among other reasons, that I may not be censured for not having performed what I never attempted. Except[36] in a very few instances the Reader will find no personifications of abstract ideas in these volumes, not that I mean to

[31] 1802: incident, which
[32] 1802: stimulation, I
[33] 1802: and,
[34] 1802: belief, that
[35] 1802: opposed, by men of greater powers,

[36] 1802 replaces Except in a very few . . . interest him likewise: by: The Reader will find that personifications of abstract ideas rarely occur in these volumes; and, I hope, are utterly rejected as an ordinary device

censure such personifications: they may be well fitted for certain sorts of composition, but in these Poems I propose to myself to imitate, and, as far as possible, to adopt the very language of men, and I do not find that such personifications make any regular or natural part of that language. I wish to keep my Reader in the company of flesh and blood, persuaded that by so doing I shall interest him. Not but that I believe that others who pursue a different track may interest him likewise:[36] I do not interfere with their claim, I only wish to prefer a different claim of my own. There will also be found in these volumes little of what is usually called poetic diction; I have taken as much pains to avoid it as others ordinarily take to produce it; this I have done for the reason already alleged, to bring my language near to the language of men, and further, because the pleasure which I have proposed to myself to impart is of a kind very different from that which is supposed by many persons to be the proper object of poetry. I do not know how without being culpably particular I can give my Reader a more exact notion of the style in which I wished these poems to be written than by informing him that I have at all times endeavoured to look steadily at my subject, consequently[37] I hope it will be found that there is[38] in these Poems little falsehood of description, and that my ideas are expressed in language fitted to their respective importance. Something I must have gained by this practice, as it is friendly to one property of all good poetry, namely[39] good sense; but it has necessarily cut me off from a large

to elevate the style, and raise it above prose. I have proposed to myself to imitate, and, as far as is possible, to adopt the very language of men; and assuredly such personifications do not make any natural or regular part of that language. They are, indeed, a figure of speech occasionally prompted by passion, and I have made use of them as such; but I have endeavoured utterly to reject them as a mechanical device of style, or as a family language which Writers in metre seem to lay claim to by prescription. I have wished to keep my Reader in the company of flesh and blood, persuaded that by so doing I shall interest him. I am, however, well aware that others who pursue a different track may interest him likewise;

[37] 1802: consequently,
[38] 1802: consequently, I hope that there is
[39] 1802: namely, good

portion of phrases and figures of speech which from father to son have long been regarded as the common inheritance of Poets. I have also thought it expedient to restrict myself still further, having abstained from the use of many expressions, in themselves proper and beautiful, but which have been foolishly repeated by bad Poets[40] till such feelings of disgust are connected with them as it is scarcely possible by any art of association to overpower.

If in a Poem there should be found a series of lines, or even a single line, in which the language, though naturally arranged and according to the strict laws of metre, does not differ from that of prose, there is a numerous class of critics[41] who, when they stumble upon these prosaisms as they call them, imagine that they have made a notable discovery, and exult over the Poet as over a man ignorant of his own profession. Now these men would establish a canon of criticism which the Reader will conclude he must utterly reject[42] if he wishes to be pleased with these volumes. And it would be a most easy task to prove to him[43] that not only the language of a large portion of every good poem, even of the most elevated character, must necessarily, except with reference to the metre, in no respect differ from that of good prose, but likewise that some of the most interesting parts of the best poems will be found to be strictly the language of prose[43] when prose is well written. The truth of this assertion might be demonstrated by innumerable passages from almost all the poetical writings, even of Milton himself. I have not space for much quotation; but, to illustrate the subject in a general manner, I will here adduce a short composition of Gray, who was at the head of those who by their reasonings have attempted to widen the space of separation betwixt Prose and Metrical composition, and was more than any other man curiously elaborate in the structure of his own poetic diction.

> In vain to me the smiling mornings shine,
> And reddening Phœbus lifts his golden fire:

---

[40] 1802: Poets, till   [41] 1802: critics,
[42] 1802: reject, if   [43] 1802: prove to him, ... of prose,

APPENDIX

> The birds in vain their amorous descant join,
> Or chearful fields resume their green attire:
> These ears alas! for other notes repine;
> *A different object do these eyes require;*
> *My lonely anguish melts no heart but mine;*
> *And in my breast the imperfect joys expire;*
> Yet Morning smiles the busy race to cheer,
> And new-born pleasure brings to happier men;
> The fields to all their wonted tribute bear;
> To warm their little loves the birds complain.
> *I fruitless mourn to him that cannot hear*
> *And weep the more because I weep in vain.*

It will easily be perceived that the only part of this Sonnet which is of any value is the lines printed in Italics: it is equally obvious[44] that[45] except in the rhyme, and in the use of the single word 'fruitless' for fruitlessly, which is so far a defect, the language of these lines does in no respect differ from that of prose.

Is there then,[46] it will be asked, no essential difference between the language of prose and metrical composition? I answer that there neither is nor can be any essential difference.[46] We are fond of tracing the resemblance between Poetry and Painting, and, accordingly, we call them Sisters: but where shall we find bonds of connection sufficiently strict to typify the affinity betwixt metrical and prose composition? They both speak by and to the same organs; the bodies in which both of them are clothed may be said to be of the same substance, their affections are kindred and almost identical, not

---

[44] 1802: obvious,   [45] 1802: that,

[46] 1802: From 'Is there then' to 'essential difference.' replaced by: By the foregoing quotation I have shewn that the language of Prose may yet be well adapted to Poetry; and I have previously asserted that a large portion of the language of every good poem can in no respect differ from that of good Prose. I will go further. I do not doubt that it may be safely affirmed, that there neither is, nor can be, any essential difference between the language of prose and metrical composition.

necessarily differing even in degree;* Poetry sheds no tears 'such as Angels weep,' but natural and human tears; she can boast of no celestial Ichor that distinguishes her vital juices from those of prose; the same human blood circulates through the veins of them both.

If it be affirmed that rhyme and metrical arrangement of themselves constitute a distinction which overturns what I have been saying on the strict affinity of metrical language with that of prose, and paves the way for other distinctions[49] which the mind voluntarily admits, I answer that[50] the distinction of rhyme and

* I here use the word 'Poetry' (though against my own judgment) as opposed to the word Prose, and synonomous with metrical composition. But much confusion has been introduced into criticism by this contradistinction of Poetry and Prose, instead of the more philosophical one of Poetry and[47] Science. The only strict antithesis to Prose is Metre.[48]

[47] 1802: of Poetry and Matter of fact, or Science.

[48] 1802: is Metre; nor is this, in truth, a *strict* antithesis; because lines and passages of metre so naturally occur in writing prose, that it would be scarcely possible to avoid them, even were it desirable.

[49] 1802: for other artificial distinctions

[50] 1802: after 'I answer that' inserts over 240 lines, dovetailing the close of the long insertion into the remainder of the sentence ('the distinction of' &c.) continued on p. 170.

I answer that the language of such Poetry as I am recommending is, as far as is possible, a selection of the language really spoken by men; that this selection, wherever it is made with true taste and feeling, will of itself form a distinction far greater than would at first be imagined, and will entirely separate the composition from the vulgarity and meanness of ordinary life; and, if metre be superadded thereto, I believe that a dissimilitude will be produced altogether sufficient for the gratification of a rational mind. What other distinction would we have? Whence is it to come? And where is it to exist? Not, surely, where the Poet speaks through the mouths of his characters: it cannot be necessary here, either for elevation of style, or any of its supposed ornaments: for, if the Poet's subject be judiciously chosen, it will naturally, and upon fit occasion, lead him to passions the language of which, if selected truly and judiciously, must necessarily be dignified and variegated, and alive with metaphors and figures. I forbear to speak of an incongruity which would shock the intelligent Reader, should the Poet interweave any foreign splendour of his own with that which the passion naturally suggests: it is sufficient to say that such addition is unnecessary. And, surely, it is more probable that those passages, which with propriety abound with metaphors and figures, will have their due effect, if, upon other occasions where the passions are of a milder character, the style also be subdued and temperate.

But, as the pleasure which I hope to give by the Poems I now present to the Reader must depend entirely on just notions upon this subject, and, as it is in itself of the highest importance to our taste and moral feelings, I cannot content myself with these detached remarks. And if, in what I am about to say, it shall appear to some that my labour is unnecessary, and that I am like a man fighting a battle without enemies, I would remind such persons, that, whatever may be the language outwardly holden by men, a practical faith in the opinions which I am wishing to establish is almost unknown. If my conclusions are admitted, and carried as far as they must be carried if admitted at all, our judgments concerning the works of the greatest Poets both ancient and modern will be far different from what they are at present, both when we praise, and when we censure: and our moral feelings influencing, and influenced by these judgments will, I believe, be corrected and purified.

Taking up the subject, then, upon general grounds, I ask what is meant by the word Poet? What is a Poet? To whom does he address himself? And what language is to be expected from him? He is a man speaking to men: a man, it is true, endued with more lively sensibility, more enthusiasm and tenderness, who has a greater knowledge of human nature, and a more comprehensive soul, than are supposed to be common among mankind; a man pleased with his own passions and volitions, and who rejoices more than other men in the spirit of life that is in him; delighting to contemplate similar volitions and passions as manifested in the goings-on of the Universe, and habitually impelled to create them where he does not find them. To these qualities he has added a disposition to be affected more than other men by absent things as if they were present; an ability of conjuring up in himself passions, which are indeed far from being the same as those produced by real events, yet (especially in those parts of the general sympathy which are pleasing and delightful) do more nearly resemble the passions produced by real events, than any thing which, from the motions of their own minds merely, other men are accustomed to feel in themselves; whence, and from practice, he has acquired a greater readiness and power in expressing what he thinks and feels, and especially those thoughts and feelings which, by his own choice, or from the structure of his own mind, arise in him without immediate external excitement.

But, whatever portion of this faculty we may suppose even the greatest Poet to possess, there cannot be a doubt but that the language which it will suggest to him, must, in liveliness and truth, fall far short of that which is uttered by men in real life, under the actual pressure of those passions, certain shadows of which the Poet thus produces, or feels to be produced, in himself. However exalted a notion we would wish to cherish of the character of a Poet, it is obvious, that, while he describes and imitates passions, his situation is altogether slavish and mechanical, compared with the freedom and power of real and substantial action and suffering. So that it will be the wish of the Poet to bring his feelings near to those of the persons whose feelings he describes, nay, for short spaces of time perhaps, to let himself slip into an entire delusion, and even confound and identify his own feelings with theirs; modifying only the language which is thus suggested to him, by a consideration that he describes for a particular purpose, that of giving pleasure. Here, then, he will apply the principle on which I have so much insisted, namely, that of selection; on this he will depend for removing what would otherwise be painful or disgusting in the passion; he will feel that there is no necessity to trick out or to elevate nature: and, the more industriously he applies this principle, the deeper will be his faith that no words, which his fancy or imagination can suggest, will be to be compared with those which are the emanations of reality and truth.

But it may be said by those who do not object to the general spirit of these remarks, that, as it is impossible for the Poet to produce upon all occasions language as exquisitely fitted for the passion as that which the real passion itself suggests, it is proper that he should consider himself as in the situation of a translator, who deems himself justified when he substitutes excellences of another kind for those which are unattainable by him; and endeavours occasionally to surpass his original, in order to make some amends for the general inferiority to which he feels that he must submit. But this would be to encourage idleness and unmanly despair. Further, it is the language of men who speak of what they do not understand; who talk of Poetry as of a matter of amusement and idle pleasure; who will converse with us as gravely about a *taste* for Poetry, as they express it, as if it were a thing as indifferent as a taste for Rope-dancing, or Frontiniac or Sherry. Aristotle, I have been told, hath said, that Poetry is the most philosophic of all writing: it is so: its object is truth, not individual and local, but general, and operative; not standing upon external testimony, but carried alive into the heart by passion; truth which is its own testimony, which gives strength and divinity to the tribunal to which it appeals, and receives them from the same tribunal. Poetry is the image of man and nature. The obstacles which stand in the way of the fidelity of the Biographer and Historian, and of their consequent utility, are incalculably greater than those which are to be encountered by the Poet who has an adequate notion of the dignity of his art. The Poet writes under one restriction only, namely, that of the necessity of giving immediate pleasure to a human Being possessed of that information which may be expected from him, not as a lawyer, a physician, a mariner, an astronomer or a natural philosopher, but as a Man. Except this one restriction, there is no object standing between the Poet and the image of things; between this, and the Biographer and Historian there are a thousand.

Nor let this necessity of producing immediate pleasure be considered as a degradation of the Poet's art. It is far otherwise. It is an acknowledgment of the beauty of the universe, an acknowledgment the more sincere because it is not formal, but indirect; it is a task light and easy to him who looks at the world in the spirit of love: further, it is a homage paid to the native and naked dignity of man, to the grand elementary principle of pleasure, by which he knows, and feels, and lives, and moves. We have no sympathy but what is propagated by pleasure: I would not be misunderstood; but wherever we sympathize with pain it will be found that the sympathy is produced and carried on by subtle combinations with pleasure. We have no knowledge, that is, no general principles drawn from the contemplation of particular facts, but what has been built up by pleasure, and exists in us by pleasure alone. The Man of Science, the Chemist and Mathematician, whatever difficulties and disgusts they may have had to struggle with, know and feel this. However painful may be the objects with which the Anatomist's knowledge is connected, he feels that his knowledge is pleasure; and where he has no pleasure he has no knowledge. What then does the Poet? He considers man and the objects that surround him as acting and re-acting upon each other, so as to produce an infinite complexity of pain and pleasure; he considers man in his own nature and in his ordinary life as contemplating this with a certain quantity of immediate knowledge, with certain convictions, intuitions, and deductions which by habit become of the nature of intuitions; he considers him as looking upon this complex scene of ideas and sensations, and finding every where objects that immediately excite in him sympathies which, from the necessities of his nature, are accompanied by an overbalance of enjoyment.

To this knowledge which all men carry about with them, and to these sympathies in which without any other discipline than that of our daily life we are fitted to take delight, the Poet principally directs his attention. He considers man and nature as essentially adapted to each other, and the mind of man as naturally the mirror of the fairest and most interesting qualities of nature. And thus the Poet, prompted by this feeling of pleasure which accompanies him through the whole course of his studies, converses with general nature with affections akin to those, which, through labour and length of time, the Man of Science has raised up in himself, by conversing with those particular parts of nature which are the objects of his studies. The knowledge both of the Poet and the Man of Science is pleasure; but the knowledge of the one cleaves to us as a necessary part of our existence, our natural and unalienable inheritance; the other is a personal and individual acquisition, slow to come to us, and by no habitual and direct sympathy connecting us with our fellow-beings. The Man of Science seeks truth as a remote and unknown benefactor; he cherishes and loves it in his solitude: the Poet, singing a song in which all human beings join with him, rejoices in the presence of truth as our visible friend and hourly companion. Poetry is the breath and finer spirit of all knowledge; it is the impassioned expression which is in the countenance of all Science. Emphatically may it be said of the Poet, as Shakespeare hath said of man, 'that he looks before and after.' He is the rock of defence of human nature; an upholder and preserver, carrying every where with him relationship and love. In spite of difference of soil and climate, of language and manners, of laws and customs, in spite of things silently gone out of mind and things violently destroyed, the Poet binds together by passion and knowledge the vast empire of human society, as it is spread over the whole earth, and over all time. The objects of the Poet's thoughts are every where; though the eyes and senses of man are, it is true, his favorite guides, yet he will follow wheresoever he can find an atmosphere of sensation in which to move his wings. Poetry is the first and last of all knowledge—it is as immortal as the heart of man. If the labours of men of Science should ever create any material revolution, direct or indirect, in our condition, and in the impressions which we habitually receive, the Poet will sleep then no more than at present, but he will be ready to follow the steps of the man of Science, not only in those general indirect effects, but he will be at his side, carrying sensation into the midst of the objects of the Science itself. The remotest discoveries of the Chemist, the Botanist, or Mineralogist, will be as proper objects of the Poet's art as any upon which it can be employed, if the time should ever come when these things shall be familiar to us, and the relations under which they are contemplated by the followers of these respective Sciences shall be manifestly and palpably material to us as enjoying and suffering beings. If the time should ever come when what is now called Science, thus familiarized to men, shall be ready to put on, as it were, a form of flesh and blood, the Poet will lend his divine spirit to aid the transfiguration, and will welcome the Being thus produced, as a dear and genuine inmate of the household of man.—It is not, then, to be supposed that any one, who holds that sublime notion of Poetry which I have attempted to convey, will break in upon the sanctity and truth of his pictures by transitory and accidental ornaments, and endeavour to excite admiration of himself by arts, the necessity of which must manifestly depend upon the assumed meanness of his subject.

What I have thus far said applies to Poetry in general; but especially to those parts of composition where the Poet speaks through the mouths of his characters; and upon this point it appears to have such weight that I will conclude, there are few persons, of good sense, who would not allow that the dramatic parts of composition are defective, in proportion as they deviate from the real language of nature, and are coloured by a diction of the Poet's own, either peculiar to him as an individual Poet, or belonging simply to Poets in general, to a body of men who, from the circumstance of their compositions being in metre, it is expected will employ a particular language.

It is not, then, in the dramatic parts of composition that we look for this distinction of language; but still it may be proper and necessary when the Poet speaks to us in his own person and character. To this I answer by referring my Reader to the description which I have before given of a Poet. Among the qualities which I have enumerated as principally conducing to form a Poet, is implied nothing differing in kind from other men, but only in degree. The sum of what I have there said is, that the Poet is chiefly distinguished from other men by a greater promptness to think and feel without immediate external excitement, and a greater power in expressing such thoughts and feelings as are produced in him in that manner. But these passions and thoughts and feelings are the general passions and thoughts and feelings of men. And with what are they connected? Undoubtedly with our moral sentiments and animal sensations, and with the causes which excite these; with the operations of the elements and the appearances of the visible universe; with storm and sun-shine, with the revolutions of the seasons, with cold and heat, with loss of friends and kindred, with injuries and resentments, gratitude and hope, with fear and sorrow. These, and the like, are the sensations and objects which the Poet describes, as they are the sensations of other men, and the objects which interest them. The Poet thinks and feels in the spirit of the passions of men. How, then, can his language differ in any material degree from that of all other men who feel vividly and see clearly? It might be *proved* that it is impossible. But supposing that this were not the case, the Poet might then be allowed to use a peculiar language, when expressing his feelings for his own gratification, or that of men like himself. But Poets do not write for Poets alone, but for men. Unless therefore we are advocates for that admiration which depends upon ignorance, and that pleasure which arises from hearing what we do not understand, the Poet must descend from this supposed height, and, in order to excite rational sympathy, he must express himself as other men express themselves. To this it may be added, that while he is only metre[51] is regular and uniform, and not,[52] like that which is produced by what is usually called poetic diction, arbitrary[53] and subject to infinite caprices upon which no calculation whatever can be made. In the one case[54] the Reader is utterly at the mercy of the Poet respecting what imagery or diction he may choose to connect with the passion, whereas in the other the metre[54] obeys certain laws, to which the Poet and Reader both willingly submit because they are certain, and because no interference is made by them with the passion but such as the concurring testimony of ages has shewn to heighten and improve the pleasure which co-exists with it.

It will now be proper to answer an obvious question, namely, why, professing these opinions[54a] have I written in verse? To this in the first place I reply,[55] because, however I may have restricted myself, there is still left open to me what confessedly constitutes the most valuable object of all writing whether in prose or verse, the great and universal passions of men, the most general and interesting of their occupations, and the entire world of nature, from which I am at liberty to supply myself with endless combinations of forms and imagery. Now, granting[56] for a moment that whatever is interesting in these objects may be as vividly described in prose, why am I to be condemned[56] if to such description I have endeavoured to superadd the charm which by the consent of all nations is acknowledged to exist in metrical language? To this[57] it will be answered, that a very small

selecting from the real language of men, or, which amounts to the same thing, composing accurately in the spirit of such selection, he is treading upon safe ground, and we know what we are to expect from him. Our feelings are the same with respect to metre; for, as it may be proper to remind the Reader,

[51-3] 1802: the distinction of metre is regular and uniform, and not like that which is produced by what is usually called poetic diction, arbitrary, and

[54] 1802: case, the ... whereas, in the other, the metre

[54a] 1802: opinions,

[55] 1802: To this, in addition to such answer as is included in what I have already said, I reply in the first place, because,

[56] 1802: Now, supposing .. condemned, if .. which, by .. nations, is

[57] 1802: To this, by such as are unconvinced by what I have already said, it may be answered,

part of the pleasure given by Poetry depends upon the metre, and that it is injudicious to write in metre[58] unless it be accompanied with the other artificial distinctions of style with which metre is usually accompanied, and that by such deviation more will be lost from the shock which will be thereby given to the Reader's associations[58] than will be counterbalanced by any pleasure which he can derive from the general power of numbers. In answer to those who thus[59] contend for the necessity of accompanying metre with certain appropriate colours of style in order to the accomplishment of its appropriate end, and who also, in my opinion, greatly under-rate the power of metre in itself, it might perhaps[60] be almost sufficient to observe that poems are extant, written upon more humble subjects, and in a more naked and simple style than[60] what I have aimed at, which poems have continued to give pleasure from generation to generation. Now, if nakedness and simplicity be a defect, the fact here mentioned affords a strong presumption that poems somewhat less naked and simple are capable of affording pleasure at the present day; and[61] all that I am now attempting is[61] to justify myself for having written under the impression of this belief.

But I might point out various causes why, when the style is manly, and the subject of some importance, words metrically arranged will long continue to impart such a pleasure to mankind as he who is sensible of the extent of that pleasure will be desirous to impart. The end of Poetry is to produce excitement in coexistence[61a] with an overbalance of pleasure. Now, by the supposition, excitement is an unusual and irregular state of the mind; ideas and feelings do not in that state succeed each other in accustomed order. But[62] if the words by which this excitement is produced are in themselves powerful, or the images and feelings have an undue proportion of pain connected

[58] 1802: metre, unless . . . associations,

[59] 1802: those who still contend

[60] 1802: it might perhaps, as far as relates to these Poems, have been almost sufficient to observe, that poems are . . . than I have aimed at,

[61] 1802: and, what I wished *chiefly* to attempt, at present, was to justify

[61a] 1802: co-existence

[62] 1802: But, if

APPENDIX

with them, there is some danger that the excitement may be carried beyond its proper bounds. Now the co-presence of something regular, something to which the mind has been accustomed when in an unexcited or[63] a less excited state, cannot but have great efficacy in tempering and restraining the passion by an intertexture[64] of ordinary feeling. This[65] may be illustrated by appealing to the Reader's own experience of the reluctance with which he comes to the re-perusal of the distressful parts of Clarissa Harlowe, or the Gamester. While Shakespeare's writings, in the most pathetic scenes, never act upon us as pathetic beyond the bounds of pleasure—an effect which[66] is in a great degree to be ascribed to small, but continual and regular impulses of pleasurable surprise from the metrical arrangement.— On the other hand (what it must be allowed will much more frequently happen) if the Poet's words should be incommensurate with the passion, and inadequate to raise the Reader to a height of desirable excitement, then, (unless the Poet's choice of his metre has been grossly injudicious) in the feelings of pleasure which the Reader has been accustomed to connect with metre in general, and in the feeling, whether chearful or melancholy, which he has been accustomed to connect with that particular movement of metre, there will be found something which will greatly contribute to impart passion

---

[63] 1802: accustomed in various moods and in a less excited state,

[64] 1802: intertexture of ordinary feeling, and of feeling not strictly and necessarily connected with the passion. This is unquestionably true, and hence, though the opinion will at first appear paradoxical, from the tendency of metre to divest language in a certain degree of its reality, and thus to throw a sort of half consciousness of unsubstantial existence over the whole composition, there can be little doubt but that more pathetic situations and sentiments, that is, those which have a greater proportion of pain connected with them, may be endured in metrical composition, especially in rhyme, than in prose. The metre of the old Ballads is very artless; yet they contain many passages which would illustrate this opinion, and, I hope, if the following Poems be attentively perused, similar instances will be found in them.

[65] 1802: This opinion may be further illustrated by appealing

[66] 1802: an effect which, in a much greater degree than might at first be imagined, is to be ascribed

to the words, and to effect the complex end which the Poet proposes to himself.

If I had undertaken a systematic defence of the theory upon which these poems are written, it would have been my duty to develope the various causes upon which the pleasure received from metrical language depends. Among the chief of these causes is to be reckoned a principle which must be well known to those who have made any of the Arts the object of accurate reflection; I mean the pleasure which the mind derives from the perception of similitude in dissimilitude. This principle is the great spring of the activity of our minds[67] and their chief feeder. From this principle the direction of the sexual appetite, and all the passions connected with it take their origin: It is the life of our ordinary conversation; and upon the accuracy with which similitude in dissimilitude, and dissimilitude in similitude are perceived, depend our taste and our moral feelings. It would not have been a useless employment to have applied this principle to the consideration of metre, and to have shewn that metre is hence enabled to afford much pleasure, and to have pointed out in what manner that pleasure is produced. But my limits will not permit me to enter upon this subject, and I must content myself with a general summary.

I have said that Poetry is the spontaneous overflow of powerful feelings: it takes its origin from emotion recollected in tranquillity: the emotion is contemplated till by a species of reaction the tranquillity gradually disappears, and an emotion,[68] similar to that which was before the subject of contemplation, is gradually produced, and does itself actually exist in the mind. In this mood successful composition generally begins, and in a mood similar to this it is carried on; but the emotion, of whatever kind and in whatever degree, from various causes is qualified by various pleasures, so that in describing any passions whatsoever, which are voluntarily described, the mind will upon the whole be in a state of enjoyment. Now[69] if Nature be thus cautious in preserving in a state of enjoyment a being thus

[67] 1802: minds,
[68] 1802: an emotion, kindred to that which
[69] 1802: Now, if

employed, the Poet ought to profit by the lesson thus held forth to him, and ought especially to take care, that whatever passions he communicates to his Reader, those passions, if his Reader's mind be sound and vigorous, should always be accompanied with an overbalance of pleasure. Now the music of harmonious metrical language, the sense of difficulty overcome, and the blind association of pleasure which has been previously received from works of rhyme or metre of the same or similar construction,[70] all these imperceptibly make up a complex feeling of delight, which is of the most important use in tempering the painful feeling which will always be found intermingled with powerful descriptions of the deeper passions. This effect is always produced in pathetic and impassioned poetry; while in lighter compositions[71] the ease and gracefulness with which the Poet manages his numbers are themselves confessedly a principal source of the gratification of the Reader. I might perhaps include all which it is *necessary* to say upon this subject by affirming what few persons will deny, that of two descriptions[72] either of passions, manners, or characters, each of them equally well executed, the one in prose and the other in verse, the verse will be read a hundred times where the prose is read once. We see that Pope by the power of verse alone, has contrived to render the plainest common sense interesting, and even frequently to invest it with the appearance of passion. In consequence of these convictions I related in metre the Tale of GOODY BLAKE and HARRY GILL, which is one of the rudest of this collection. I wished to draw attention to the truth that the power of the human imagination is sufficient to produce such changes even in our physical nature as might almost appear miraculous. The truth is an important one; the fact (for it is a *fact*) is a valuable illustration of it. And I have the satisfaction of knowing that it has been communicated to many hundreds of people who would never have heard of it, had it not

[70] 1802: similar construction, an indistinct perception perpetually renewed of language closely resembling that of real life, and yet, in the circumstance of metre, differing from it so widely, all these

[71] 1802: while, in lighter compositions, the ease

[72] 1802: affirming, . . . that, of two descriptions, either

APPENDIX 175

been narrated as a Ballad, and in a more impressive metre than is usual in Ballads.

Having thus adverted to[73] a few of the reasons why I have written in verse, and why I have chosen subjects from common life, and endeavoured to bring my language near to the real language of men, if I have been too minute in pleading my own cause, I have at the same time been treating a subject of general interest; and it is for this reason that I request the Reader's permission to add a few words with reference solely to these particular poems, and to some defects which will probably be found in them. I am sensible that my associations must have sometimes been particular instead of general, and that, consequently, giving to things a false importance, sometimes from diseased impulses I may have written upon unworthy subjects; but I am less apprehensive on this account, than that my language may frequently have suffered from those arbitrary connections of feelings and ideas with particular[74] words, from which no man can altogether protect himself. Hence I have no doubt[75] that in some instances[75] feelings even of the ludicrous may be given to my Readers by expressions which appeared to me tender and pathetic. Such faulty expressions, were I convinced they were faulty at present, and that they must necessarily continue to be so, I would willingly take all reasonable pains to correct. But it is dangerous to make these alterations on the simple authority of a few individuals, or even of certain classes of men; for where the understanding of an Author is not convinced, or his feelings altered, this cannot be done without great injury to himself: for his own feelings are his stay and support, and[76] if he sets them aside in one instance, he may be induced to repeat this act till his mind loses all confidence in itself[76] and becomes utterly debilitated. To this it may be added, that the Reader ought never to forget that he is himself exposed to the same errors as the Poet, and perhaps in a much greater degree: for there can be no presumption in saying[77] that it is not probable he will be so well acquainted with

[73] 1802: Having thus explained a few
[74] 1802: particular words and phrases, from which
[75] 1802: Hence I have no doubt, that, . . . instances,
[76] 1802: and, . . . itself,   [77] 1802: in saying, that

the various stages of meaning through which words have passed, or with the fickleness or stability of the relations of particular ideas to each other; and above all, since he is so much less interested in the subject, he may decide lightly and carelessly.

Long as I have detained my Reader, I hope he will permit me to caution him against a mode of false criticism which has been applied to Poetry in which the language closely resembles that of life and nature. Such verses have been triumphed over in parodies of which Dr. Johnson's Stanza is a fair specimen.

> 'I put my hat upon my head,
> And walk'd into the Strand,
> And there I met another man
> Whose hat was in his hand.'

Immediately under these lines I will place one of the most justly admired stanzas of the '*Babes* in the Wood.'

> 'These pretty Babes with hand in hand
> Went wandering up and down;
> But never more they saw the Man
> Approaching from the Town.'

In both[78] of these stanzas the words, and the order of the words, in no respect differ from the most unimpassioned conversation. There are words in both, for example, 'the Strand,' and 'the Town,' connected with none but the most familiar ideas; yet the one stanza we admit as admirable, and the other as a fair example of the superlatively contemptible. Whence arises this difference? Not from the metre, not from the language, not from the order of the words; but the *matter* expressed in Dr. Johnson's stanza is contemptible. The proper method of treating trivial and simple verses to which Dr. Johnson's stanza would be a fair parallelism is not to say[79] this is a bad kind of poetry, or this is not poetry,[80] but this wants sense; it is neither interesting in itself, nor can *lead* to any thing interesting; the images neither originate in that sane state of feeling which arises out of thought, nor can excite thought or feeling in the Reader.

[78] 1802: In both these stanzas   [79] 1802: not to say, this is
[80] 1802: poetry; but this wants ... man?

This is the only sensible manner of dealing with such verses: Why trouble yourself about the species till you have previously decided upon the genus? Why take pains to prove that an Ape is not a Newton when it is self-evident that he is not a man.[80]

I have one request to make of my Reader, which is, that in judging these Poems he would decide by his own feelings genuinely, and not by reflection upon what will probably be the judgment of others. How common is it to hear a person say, 'I myself do not object to this style of composition or this or that expression, but to such and such classes of people it will appear mean or ludicrous.' This mode of criticism[81] so destructive of all sound unadulterated judgment[82] is almost universal: I have therefore to request[83] that the Reader would abide independently by his own feelings, and that if he finds himself affected he would not suffer such conjectures to interfere with his pleasure.

If an Author by any single composition has impressed us with respect for his talents, it is useful to consider this as affording a presumption, that, on other occasions where we have been displeased, he nevertheless may not have written ill or absurdly; and, further, to give him so much credit for this one composition as may induce us to review what has displeased us with more care than we should otherwise have bestowed upon it. This is not only an act of justice, but in our decisions upon poetry especially, may conduce in a high degree to the improvement of our own taste: for an *accurate* taste in Poetry[84] and in all the other arts, as Sir Joshua Reynolds has observed, is an *acquired* talent, which can only be produced by thought and a long continued intercourse with the best models of composition. This is mentioned[85] not with so ridiculous a purpose as to prevent the most inexperienced Reader from judging for himself, (I have already said that I wish him to judge for himself;) but merely to temper the rashness of decision, and to suggest[85] that if Poetry be a subject on which

[81] 1802: criticism, so
[82] 1802: judgment, is
[83] 1802: request,
[84] 1802: poetry, and
[85] 1802: mentioned, . . . suggest, that, if . . . erroneous; and that

much time has not been bestowed, the judgment may be erroneous,[85] and that in many cases it necessarily will be so.

I know that nothing would have so effectually contributed to further the end which I have in view as to have shewn of what kind the pleasure is, and how the pleasure is produced[86] which is confessedly produced by metrical composition essentially different from what I have here endeavoured to recommend;[86] for the Reader will say that he has been pleased by such composition[86] and what can I do more for him? The power of any art is limited[87] and he will suspect that if I propose to furnish him with new friends it is only upon condition of his abandoning his old friends. Besides, as I have said, the Reader is himself conscious of the pleasure which he has received from such composition, composition to which he has peculiarly attached the endearing name of Poetry; and all men feel an habitual gratitude, and something of an honorable bigotry for the objects which have long continued to please them: we not only wish to be pleased, but to be pleased in that particular way in which we have been accustomed to be pleased. There is a host of arguments in these feelings; and I should be the less able to combat them successfully, as I am willing to allow, that, in order entirely to enjoy the Poetry which I am recommending, it would be necessary to give up much of what is ordinarily enjoyed. But[88] would my limits have permitted me to point out how this pleasure is produced, I might have removed many obstacles, and assisted my Reader in perceiving that the powers of language are not so limited as he may suppose; and that it is possible that poetry may give other enjoyments, of a purer, more lasting, and more exquisite nature. But this[89] part of my subject I have been obliged altogether to omit: as it has been less my present aim to prove that the interest excited by some other kinds of poetry is less vivid, and less worthy of the nobler powers of the mind,

[86] 1802: how that pleasure is produced, which is confessedly ... recommend: for ... composition; and what

[87] 1802: limited; and he will suspect, that, ... new friends, it is

[88] 1802: But, would

[89] 1802: This part of my subject I have not altogether neglected; but it has been less my present aim to prove, that

than to offer reasons for presuming, that, if the object which I have proposed to myself were adequately attained, a species of poetry would be produced, which is genuine poetry; in its nature well adapted to interest mankind permanently, and likewise important in the multiplicity and quality of its moral relations.

From what has been said, and from a perusal of the Poems, the Reader will be able clearly to perceive the object which I have proposed to myself: he will determine how far I have attained this object; and, what is a much more important question, whether it be worth attaining; and upon the decision of these two questions will rest my claim to the approbation of the public.

ADDENDA

P. 51, l. 31. In March 1796 Dorothy Wordsworth remarks on Dorsetshire as 'a country where coals are so expensive' (*E.Y.*, p. 166).

P. 102, ll. 23–24. An echo of the famous lines of Denham's *Cooper's Hill*, frequently praised by critics and imitated during the eighteenth century:

> O could I flow like thee [the Thames], and make thy stream
> My great example, as it is my theme!
> Though deep, yet clear; though gentle, yet not dull;
> Strong without rage, without o'er-flowing full. (189–92)

P. 110, l. 9. thick-ribbed] The only example given in *O.E.D.* is Shakespeare, *Measure for Measure*, III. i. 120–1: 'to reside In thrilling region of thick-ribbed ice'. Cf. *Prel.*, I. 517: 'A thick-ribbed army', used jocularly of the [? court] cards of a dilapidated pack.

DATE DUE

MAR 17 '77			
GAYLORD			PRINTED IN U.S.A.